# TERESA OF THE POOR

# Teresa of the Poor

*The Story of Her Life*

## RENZO ALLEGRI

CHARIS
Servant Publications
Ann Arbor, Michigan

Charis Books is an imprint of Servant Publications
especially designed to serve Roman Catholics.

Published by Servant Publications
P.O. Box 8617
Ann Arbor, Michigan 48107

Cover design: Left Coast Design, Inc., Portland, Oregon
Cover photo: Mirror Syndication International, London, England

    99  00  01  10  9  8  7  6  5  4  3  2

Printed in the United States of America
ISBN 1-56955-100-6

LIBRARY OF CONGRESS CATALOGING-IN-PUBLICATION DATA

Allegri, Renzo.
    [Teresa dei poveri.  English]
    Teresa of the poor : the story of her life / Renzo Allegri.
        p.    cm.
    ISBN 1-56955-100-6
    1. Teresa, Mot6her, 1910-1997  .   2. Missionaries of
Charity—Biography.    3. Nuns—India—Calcutta—Biography.
I. Title.
BX4406.5.Z8Z5513  1996
271'.97—dc20                                                      95-45951
    [B]                                                                CIP

To my Friend
Natale Ramoni,
a doctor,
who prematurely died,
who practiced his profession
with loving availability,
with wise competency
and with unforgettable humanity
especially toward the poor.

# Contents

# O N E

# RESTING AMONG
# THE PEOPLE SHE LOVED

Since September 13, 1997, Mother Teresa's body has been resting in a tomb in the heart of Calcutta. It is located on the ground floor of the motherhouse of the Missionaries of Charity, the religious congregation she founded, the place where she began her mission among the poorest of the poor in the late 1940s.

Hers is a simple, white cement tomb, devoid of any ornamentation. A verse from the Gospel of St. John is carved on a marble slab, summing up the spirit of service that characterized Mother Teresa's life: "Love one another as I have loved you." There is a black cross underneath, followed by the words, "Mother Teresa 27/8/1910–5/9/1997, our dear and beloved founding Mother."

The tomb is located in a room that was once the sisters' refectory, a large room with windows that overlook one of Calcutta's busiest and poorest streets, Lower Circular Road. The deafening noise of the traffic, the odor of smog, the stench of the perpetually clogged sewers, and the humidity from the seasonal rains all enter the room from outside. This is the Calcutta that Mother Teresa loved, the Calcutta of the poor, of the ordinary, of the sick, the handicapped, and the wretched.

These same people, individually or in little groups, continue to flow into this room throughout the day and stand in front of Mother Teresa's tomb. They pray, or according to an Indian religious custom, they speak with her mortal remains, as if she were still there listening to them. Each one seeks some kind of physical contact, whether it be putting a flower on her tomb or lightly rubbing the marble slab.

Rumor has it that it was not easy for the Missionaries of Charity to obtain permission to bury Mother Teresa in their residence. Indian law prohibits keeping bodies in private homes. But for the little "saint" of Calcutta, the government made an exception. There was no place more appropriate for her eternal repose than her own home, where she worked for half a century among the people she loved.

Both the government of India and the hierarchy of the Catholic Church joined together in devote homage during her funeral ceremony, which took place on September 13, 1997. In the morning, the Indian government organized a large procession that paraded through the streets of the city en route to Netaji Stadium, and that accompanied Mother Teresa's body as it lay on a the military gun carriage that once bore the bodies of Mahatma Gandhi and Jawaharlal Nehru. Catholic church authorities, joined by leaders from three other religions, watched in respectful silence. The entire funeral ceremony, which lasted six hours, was broadcast on television around the world. Then, in the afternoon, Mother Teresa's body was laid to rest among her people, her extended family, the poor who had always been her neighbors. A banner, hoisted on the facade of a building that overlooks the motherhouse of the sisters, said: "Mother, you have gone away but we'll never forget you. Your neighbors."

In life, Mother Teresa was one of the world's best known women. Certainly history will remember her always as one of the most influential religious figures of the Catholic church in the second half of the twentieth century—all without having the benefit of offices, palaces, residences, secretaries, or telephones, but always working from the street. Mother Teresa lived in poverty just like the people she helped. It was appropriate, therefore, that, even after her death, she should return to the edge of that noisy street in the heart of Calcutta to repose in the midst of those who have nothing.

Mother Teresa's extraordinary life on earth began right in that street, seemingly as a whim or as the result of some mad folly. Her decision did not fall into any category of rational thinking; she abandoned herself to divine foolhardiness.

Only after her death did people understand that her gesture was an unyielding act of faith in the gospel, an immense act of love. Mother Teresa, who was thirty-six at the time of her decision to take up that life, had truly fallen in love, and like everyone who has fallen in love, had acted on an impulse, following the dictates of her heart.

That love never wavered, and Mother Teresa always lived like someone who was in love. And with her love, she accomplished extraordinary wonders. She became the greatest symbol of those virtues that ennoble mankind: namely, generosity, altruism, and love.

Popes, heads of states, rulers, governors, artists, intellectuals—a host of people belonging to all races, religions, and ideologies—admired her, and continue to do so. "Mother Teresa is an angel," people often wrote. "In her presence," Indira Gandhi once said, "we feel lowly and ashamed of ourselves."

The world has honored her with its most prestigious

awards. In 1963, India presented her with its highest award, the Padmashree (Magnificient Lotus) Award. That same year the Philippine government gave her the Magsaysay Award for International Understanding. In 1971, she received the Pope John XXIII Peace Prize from Pope Paul VI. A few months later, an American group in Boston presented her with the Good Samaritan Award. In 1972 the Indian government, after having already given her the Padmashree Award, honored her with the Pandit Nehru Award for International Understanding. In 1973, based on her outstanding religious witness, the Prince of Edinburgh awarded her the Templeton Prize for Progress in Religion, an honor for which a jury of ten representatives from as many worldwide religious groups unanimously chose her from among two thousand candidates of various nationalities and religions. In 1975, the United Nations Organization for Food and Agriculture (FAO) honored her with the Albert Schweitzer Prize "as an expression of gratitude for her untiring dedication to the hungry and poor of the entire world." In 1979, she received first the Balzan International Prize of $325,000 in Rome and then the Nobel Peace Prize of $190,000 in Oslo.

Her honorary degrees were numerous. Possibly no other woman in the twentieth century has been more celebrated and more acclaimed than she has. Nevertheless, Mother Teresa always remained incredibly humble and modest. "I am nothing," she always said.

I had the good fortune to meet her on different occasions, to travel by car with her, and to spend hours in conversation with her. She spoke to me about God, about Jesus, about spiritual life, and about her work, which continues to reach out to the whole world. Even though she was reluctant to touch upon topics concerning her life, she did, however, talk about her childhood and youth. She told me how her own vocation of service to the poorest of the poor was born and how it developed.

My meetings with Mother Teresa constitute a particularly significant moment in my life. Her words are deeply impressed on my mind and will always remain so. They were also recorded in my notes and on tape. I had always wanted to gather them together and organize them in a brief and concise account of this extraordinary nun's life. Thus, a little book has evolved that, instead of being a true and proper biography of Mother Teresa, is the chronicle of a long meeting between a journalist and a great "saint" of our time.

# T W O

# POPE PAUL VI'S GIFT

The first time I heard about Mother Teresa was in 1971. On January 6 of that year, she arrived in Rome to receive the Pope John XXIII Peace Prize from Pope Paul VI, a prestigious award of $25,000—a good amount at the time. Newspapers reported this news but did not highlight it since Mother Teresa was not yet very well known in Italy.

A few months later I read a report from Calcutta in a weekly magazine in which the writer reconstructed the story of Mother Teresa's work in India. He wrote of her helping the poorest of the poor and, above all, of the hospital that she had opened for the dying.

It was this latter initiative, a unique and humanitarian thing to do, that amazed me. Calcutta is an immense city with countless inhabitants, where misery seems to have no limits. Poor people die here, totally abandoned on the sidewalks, and even more so at the time when Mother Teresa first opened her hospital for the dying. At that time, too, thousands of Pakistani refugees and tens of thousands of displaced families who had lost everything in a terrible cyclone that had ravaged southwest Bengal had joined the throngs of homeless people who were roaming the city. These people were wandering around famished, succumbing to horrible diseases, and dying totally abandoned in the streets.

Mother Teresa wanted to help them. She especially

suffered when she saw people dying in the streets. She wanted them to be able to die stretched out on a bed, with someone close by who would care for them. "They are God's children and they should die with a smile on their lips," she said. For this reason, she had opened her hospital.

Every morning Mother Teresa and her young sisters went about the city, gathering up the dying who lay abandoned on the sidewalks. Bringing them to their hospital, the sisters washed them, put them in beds, and lovingly cared for them until they breathed their last.

It was a marvelous yet disconcerting fact. This nun was taking care of people who, in the world's eyes, were the least important: not only the destitute but the dying; people whose lives were coming to an end. She received them warmly and devoted herself to them so that they might die with dignity. Those whom she saved were neither children with an entire life ahead of them nor young people who might someday be useful to society. They were the old and hopelessly dying, lepers consumed by their disease, broken human beings. Prolonging their lives by even a day served no purpose—except, perhaps, to prolong their suffering. At least this is what we may think.

But Mother Teresa thought differently. To her, these "broken human beings" were God's children, her beloved brothers and sisters, and she did not want them to leave this world without knowing that someone cared about their well-being.

This particularly remained engraved in my mind. I continued to reflect on it. I wondered how such an idea had occurred to her. I thought it was an interesting and edifying effort. I found it downright poetic, belonging to that sublime poetry that is at the source of life. But her effort seemed hardly practical. Mother Teresa and her sisters

were wasting precious time with those dying people, time
that they could have devoted to abandoned children who,
with some help, could be saved, could live longer.

Hoping to better grasp the meaning behind this
woman's actions, I read again the article about her receiving the Pope John XXIII Peace Prize. I was especially
intrigued by Pope Paul VI's reasons for awarding it to her:

> We offer you with great pleasure and for the first time
> ever the "Peace Prize" dedicated to Pope John XXIII,
> instituted to celebrate World Peace Day in 1971, and
> awarded on the Feast of the Epiphany in the presence
> of members of the diplomatic corps that is accredited to
> the Holy See and members of the Roman Curia. We
> instituted it to honor the memory of our venerable pre-
> decessor, Pope John XXIII, in order to serve the cause
> for peace and encourage those who are dedicating their
> lives to helping people spiritually and corporally.
> Recalling our unforgettable pilgrimage to India, we
> invoke from the depths of our hearts every divine grace
> on this work of charity that you sustain so generously
> every day, and we impart to you our apostolic blessing.
> Vatican City, January 6, 1971. Signed Paulus P.P. VI.

I read and reread these reasons. They contained phrases
that popes rarely use when speaking about living persons.
As Pope Paul VI says in his text, it was the first time that
this award was given out. Therefore the pope wanted to
choose an exceptional, extraordinary person to hold up as
an example to the world, and he chose a humble sister
who was working in India. Moreover, popes know their
words remain written in history, which makes them very
cautious. Their expressions are measured, pondered, and
examined. As a rule, they always say a lot less than they

really would admit. Yet Pope Paul VI was freer in his words than perhaps he had ever been. He singled out Mother Teresa as an example to all those in the world who are "dedicating their lives to helping people spiritually and corporally." In essence he was saying that she was simply a marvelous woman who behaved like a true saint, and that she is an example for all Christians.

Pope Paul VI's attitude was revealing. It showed he had tremendous admiration for her, so great as to defy the powerful Roman Curia, which would most likely have not approved such a declaration of praise for a living person.

The Pope also alluded to his trip to India in December of 1964. He had been pope for barely two years when he went to Bombay for the close of the 38th International Eucharistic Congress that was being held there; he wanted to meet Mother Teresa. At the end of their meeting, he showed his admiration and appreciation for her with a sensational gesture that caught the attention of the world-wide press.

On that occasion a rich American industrialist had given the Pope the gift of a beautiful white car with red seats, a Lincoln that cost $5,500 at that time. At the close of the Eucharistic Congress as he was leaving Bombay, Paul VI said: "We donate our white car to Mother Teresa, to help her in her universal mission of love."

From that time on, it was evident that Paul VI knew and appreciated that unusual sister who, out of love for God, wanted to make it possible for destitute people in Calcutta to die with a smile upon their lips.

Reading all these things, my curiosity grew. Because of the richness of her spirit, I felt this nun was an exceptional woman and an extraordinary subject for a journalist. I wanted to meet her and interview her.

But, as I already said, Mother Teresa was not very well

known in Italy at the time, and newspapers were not very interested in what was happening with her.

In 1973, Mother Teresa traveled to Milan. She was invited by the Pontifical Institute for Foreign Missions to take part in a rally for young people who were working in missions. Youth in the area responded enthusiastically to this event. A crowd of ten thousand young people gathered around Milan's famous Duomo, and Mother Teresa was among them in the front row. I was able to observe her at that time. It was March and cold in Milan, yet she wore only a white sari with a plain wool cardigan on top. Her feet were bare except for some rough, heavy leather sandals.

The event organizers had invited her to address the rally before they began their parade through the city. She walked up to the microphone and simply said, "Let each of us do our part. You use your feet, and I'll use my knees. While you are walking, I'll be praying for your footsteps." The procession of young people moved on. Mother Teresa went into a church near the Piazza Duomo, began to pray, and remained there until the rally ended.

The next day the mayor of Milan received Mother Teresa at city hall and awarded her the Ambrogino Medal, an award for people of good merit. "Look, it's pure gold," the master of ceremonies said. Mother Teresa answered, "Then I'll have to give it to someone who's hungry."

From that moment on, newspapers in Italy were writing more about Mother Teresa. I found out she had already opened a house in Rome, and my desire to meet her grew even more. But several years passed before my dream came true.

# T H R E E

# "I WANT NOTHING"

In 1975 I went to Rome to interview Bishop Paul Hnilica, a Slovak bishop who had miraculously fled the communist persecution in his country. He is an extraordinary person who, though forced to live in exile for many years, organized various efforts to continue his apostolic mission in the countries of Eastern Europe through clandestine, yet very efficient, channels.

While speaking with him, I learned that he knew Mother Teresa very well. He was the one who drew Pope Paul VI's attention to her extraordinary charitable activities, and he was the one who offered her hospitality in Rome when the Pope asked her to come and open one of her houses in the Eternal City.

"Can I meet Mother Teresa?" I asked Bishop Hnilica at once. From our first meeting this simple Slovak bishop told me to forget any formalities and to simply call him Fr. Paul. He usually dressed like an ordinary priest and almost never wore the insignia of a bishop. His house was always full of needy people, whether they were refugees from the Iron Curtain countries or simply homeless people off the street. He met them on the street, where they asked him for alms. Instead of handing them some change, the bishop stopped to talk with them, asked them about their families, and frequently brought them home, where he fed them and gave them a place to sleep while they looked for work and housing. He, too, was a sort of Mother

Teresa. "Can I meet this sister?" I repeated insistently.

"Of course," Bishop Hnilica responded with his joyful voice. "If you write an article about her and her work, it could be useful. She has a lot going. Here in Rome she has already opened two houses for the poor, but there are additional needs. Newspaper articles form public opinion. People aren't insensitive. When she knows there are people out there who are interested in the poor and who will give generously, she's ready to help. I know that for sure. You'll see that you'll also be able to help. When Mother Teresa comes to Rome, I'll call you and we'll set up a meeting."

Bishop Hnilica is a volcano of ideas. His mind never stops. He thinks and acts with the spontaneity of those who madly believe in God. For him, anything is possible, provided that it is worthy. At that time his secretary and collaborator was Fr. Sergio Mercanzin, a young and intelligent priest from Venice. I commended myself to him too. Both reassured me. I thought the meeting with this extraordinary sister would be confirmed within a few weeks, but instead I had to wait several years.

Mother Teresa did not like interviews. It was not because she did not like journalists, only that she did not like to talk about herself. "I'm simply an instrument in God's hands," she said repeatedly. "If I've done something good, it's not to my credit. I've only carried out the Lord's inspiration as best as I could. So you shouldn't speak about me but about the work the Lord has inspired me to do."

I did not want a formal meeting with her. Nor did I want to be introduced to her so I could take advantage of the opportunity to ask her some questions and force some answers out of her. I was not interested in such an interview. I wanted to be able to talk with her peacefully, win her trust, and get her to confide in me about her life, her extraordinary work, and the feelings and emotions she experienced as she worked among those rejected by humanity. In short, I wanted to get to know this exceptional woman as deeply as possible through some brief encounters, and have the good fortune of penetrating the depths of her heart and of her soul at least a little. I wanted to "spy" into the heart and soul of a saint.

Maybe that desire was sacrilegious but the intentions were good. I was sure that much good would be done by telling people what I would learn from this woman, telling it with all the emotion that I would have from such an extraordinary experience. I would help raise many people's awareness by getting them to reflect on her ideals, thereby inspiring them to give generously to those who have nothing. So I asked Bishop Hnilica to convey my intentions to Mother Teresa, convinced that she would understand and grant me an appointment.

We journalists are accustomed to dealing mainly with people who seek to benefit from our profession. Politicians, actors, singers, industrialists, businessmen, writers, poets, painters, and lawyers are all people who smugly remind themselves that "publicity is the soul of business" when they find themselves in a journalist's presence. They respond to every question with pleasure. They even do it when they know they are at a disadvantage. They realize that the answers they give to a journalist can work to their advantage, and that they can "profit" from an interview. They only refuse an interview to raise the price: either they attach some conditions to it that will put them in a better position to defend their viewpoint, or they try to get more money out of it.

Even churchmen are not strangers to this mentality. They, too, know that publicity is very useful, and when they have the occasion they take advantage of it. As a matter of fact, they very often seek it out.

In my long career as a journalist, I have rarely found a person who has refused an interview. I can recall famous actors, rich industrialists, and powerful politicians who not only quickly set up an appointment with me, but sent a car to fetch me at my office and offered me hospitality in their villas. They did so not because they highly respected me, but simply because my interview with them would be free publicity for their business, their ideas, or their vanity.

One of the few people who was absolutely oblivious to this was Mother Teresa. My bishop friend was convinced that an interview would help make her work more widely known and raise some additional funds. Every time Mother Teresa came to Rome, he told her this and added that she could trust me as a journalist because he knew me and had observed my professional honesty on many occasions. But Mother Teresa remained absolutely indifferent. She said that she had many responsibilities and did not have any time for meeting with a journalist. She also said that she did not want people talking about her. But since she was a very kind person, she added that perhaps the interview could be done at another time when she was in Rome and things were quieter.

It was only later, when I had the fortune of meeting her, that I was able to see how different Mother Teresa's parameters of thinking were from those of other people. One day, when she was talking about how people could help, she told me that she had never in her life asked anyone for offerings. "My work," she told me, "is the work the Lord desires. He is the one who has to be interested in keeping it alive. When he no longer gives me what is needed, it means that the work no longer serves him. I pray, but I don't ask for anyone's special intervention."

One day Bishop Hnilica called me to say that he had

set up an appointment with Mother Teresa. I immediately caught a plane to Rome.

The next morning, accompanied by Bishop Hnilica and Fr. Sergio Mercanzin, I went to Casilina on the outskirts of Rome, where one of the houses of Mother Teresa's congregation of sisters is located. Mother Teresa was waiting for me at the entrance. She greeted me and warmly shook my hand. We sat around a table under a big tree.

"What can I tell you?" asked Mother Teresa, looking at me with a marvelous smile on her lips.

"I would like you to tell me about yourself and your marvelous work with the poorest of the poor in the world," I said, trying to break the ice. After I had said the words, "your marvelous work with the poorest of the poor," I immediately realized how ridiculous my request sounded and turned red from embarrassment. Mother Teresa noticed that I was embarrassed. I could tell by the way she looked at me. She must have understood how embarrassed I was, because she was extremely kind and loving toward me. Those who were with me noticed this and told me the same thing afterward.

"There's nothing to say about me," she insisted. "I'm a poor sister like so many others. The Lord has entrusted a mission to me and I try to do it as best I can. But he is the one who does everything. Jesus loves the poor. They're his beloved sons and daughters. Even he was born into a poor family when he came into this world, and the most beautiful words of the Gospel are reserved for the poor. It's necessary to talk about them and not me. I am worth nothing."

She spoke with enthusiasm, but without emphasis. Her tone was subdued and intimate, and her voice was sweet and persuasive. Sitting there in front of me, Mother Teresa seemed very small, much smaller than I had imagined, and very thin. Her shoulders were rounded. She was sitting, but seemed rolled up into a ball on the chair. To look at me she had to lift her head, and she did so with difficulty because her shoulders, stiff from arthritis, forced her to bend her head forward. Probably this movement was painful, but no one could tell. When she looked at me, I saw eyes that were as clear as a child's. Her hands, though, were knobby, contorted, and worn out from toiling. Her feet, with their heavy and coarse sandals, appeared painfully deformed by the thousands of miles she had walked over dust, mud, and stones. For more than forty years Mother Teresa had been constantly moving about, bringing help to the suffering. In rain or shine, she always went around on foot, smiling and praying. Now her feet were deformed by the enormous work she had done.

"When do you remember having a vocation to be a nun?" I asked.

"The Lord's call is a mystery," she answered. "Maybe it's only when we're in paradise that we'll be able to know the deepest 'whys' of our life. I believe I first felt a clear call from the Lord for living a life dedicated to him around twelve years of age. I was living with my family in Skopje. My mother was a deeply Christian woman; maybe her example and her love for the poor had a decisive influence on me. But at the time, I didn't want to be a nun. It's only much later that I answered the Lord's call, when I was eighteen."

# F O U R

# HER FAMILY'S SECRET

Mother Teresa almost never talked about her family.

Whenever anyone asked her precise questions about her childhood and youth, she always gave short, generic, and somewhat evasive answers. Often she did not answer directly, giving the impression that, perhaps for some secret reason, she did not want to broach the topic.

In reality, her silence and discretion on her distant past were rooted in a significant family drama involving the death of her father, who was killed for political reasons when he was still young, and the suffering of her mother, who remained practically a prisoner of the communist regime until her death. Mother Teresa was strongly attached to her parents, and suffered much because of their plight. But she also found the immense strength to forgive, and for this reason did not like to recall her past and make any judgments on what had happened.

It was Lazar, her older brother, who revealed the behind-the-scenes intrigue involving the family. Lazar moved to Italy at the end of World War II and spent the rest of his life in Palermo, where he was the director of a branch office of a large pharmaceutical company. He died there in 1981. When Mother Teresa was awarded the Nobel Peace Prize in 1979 and the press was saying that she was of Slavic background, he decided to reveal the truth about his family and recount their dramatic story. When he did, it finally became clear why Mother Teresa was always evasive when journalists asked her about her past.

During those years when Mother Teresa was becoming a popular personality because of her great humanitarian work in India, her mother and sister were living in Tirana, Albania. A rigid and fiercely atheistic regime existed in Albania. Mother Teresa evaded every detail regarding her background out of fear that it might create problems for her mother and sister. She knew that they were living in dreadful conditions. For years she secretly tried to obtain permission for the two women to leave the country, but all her efforts were in vain. She never saw them again.

When Communism faded away, it was possible to describe in detail this period of Mother Teresa's life. Her parents' example, especially her mother's, influenced the choice of this great "saint" of Calcutta, and so this period of her life was an important part of the formation of her vocation.

Agnes Bojaxhiu (her family nickname is "Gonxha," which means "flower bud") was born on August 27, 1910 in Skopje, Yugoslavia. One might therefore deduce that Mother Teresa is a Slav. But this is not the case. She is Albanian. Skopje is a border town that has passed from state to state in the course of history. It has been annexed to Turkey and to Serbia but its origins are Albanian. In fact, most of the inhabitants of Skopje speak Albanian; the Bojaxhius felt Albanian and spoke Albanian.

Mother Teresa was born into a well-to-do and religious family. Her father, Nicola Bojaxhiu, was a prosperous businessman with a degree in pharmacy. He also had a construction business and built Skopje's first theater. Her mother, Drone (the name of a flower in Albania), also came from a wealthy family. She married when she was fifteen, eighteen years younger than her husband. By sixteen years of age, she was already the mother of their first daughter, Agatha. At eighteen, she had a son, Lazar. She was almost twenty when the future Mother Teresa was born.

The Bojaxhiu family was happy and united. They resided in a beautiful home with a large garden always full of flowers. The family had another house in the garden that was reserved for guests and relatives.

The population of Skopje was mainly Muslim at that time. There was a significant Greek Orthodox population, but Catholics were few. The Bojaxhius belonged to this small minority.

As is almost always the case of those who belong to a minority, the Bojaxhius were proud of their faith and practiced it with enthusiasm, consistency, and zeal. As the mother of the family, Drone took great responsibility for the education of her children. She was very religious and diligently passed on to her children the faith that she had received from her parents.

There was a small chapel a few steps away from the Bojaxhius' home. Drone took her three children there to pray and attend mass every morning when Nicola left for work. As dusk settled in the evening, Drone would gather the family in the living room to pray the rosary together. This was a very important time in the day, and any guests or relatives who were staying in the guest house were invited to join them.

Drone lived her faith simply and concretely. Following the teaching of the gospel, she took it upon herself to love others in deeds. She remembered the words of Jesus: "Whatever you do for the poor out of love for me, you do unto me." Being a good Christian, she had the custom of going once a week to visit the sick and of taking food and clothing to the poor. Even though her children were little, they would accompany her. "You are fortunate," she told them. "You have a beautiful house, food, and clothing. You don't lack anything. But you must not forget that many people suffer from hunger and that there are children who don't have anything to wear and, when they get sick, don't have medicine to make them well."

Lazar Bojaxhiu told me that Agnes, the future Mother Teresa, was the one who most enthusiastically followed their mother's religious advice. Lazar gave me one example of this:

There was a poor widow who lived with her seven children, almost all of whom were little, in a dark and dirty room. Our hearts would break whenever we visited them with our mother and saw those poor creatures crowded together on one big bed that was a sort of pallet with dirty and worn out blankets. They had one little room for eight people, a tiny cubbyhole for a kitchen, and no bathroom, while we each had a beautiful bedroom and a bathtub with running water—a rarity in Skopje back then. My sister Agatha and I never went to their house on our own, but Agnes was almost always there with those dirty and malnourished children. When she got out of school for lunch, she would stop and visit them before returning to the house. Then she would return in the afternoon to have a snack with them. Of course, she took the snack. Later, when that poor woman died, her children practically lived in our house.

Drone's example must have made a deep impression on young Agnes' heart. Once when speaking about her own vocation, Mother Teresa said: "I wouldn't be able to say whether my mother's example and her love for the poor or my frequent attendance at church had the most influence on me as my vocation matured."

Peace and tranquility did not last long for the Bojaxhiu family. Nicola was involved in politics. He was fighting for the rights of the population of the Kosovo region, which was Albanian and wished to remain Albanian.

In 1913 Albania obtained its independence and the Bojaxhius celebrated. But immediately afterward, the country was divided and the Kosovo region became part of Yugoslavia even though the people of the region wanted to remain under Albanian rule. As a result, the region was a continual hotbed of tension and revolt that troops from Belgrade violently put down. Troops especially singled out those who had influence over the people. Among them was Agnes' father, whom people throughout the city held in high esteem and respect.

Thus, Yugoslav authorities began to persecute Nicola Bojaxhiu. They attacked him with a vengeance. They began to sabotage his work by every means possible. His business experienced great difficulties and was on the verge of bankruptcy. But Nicola did not give up. Then the Yugoslavian authorities took more drastic measures. As Lazar Bojaxhiu remembers,

In 1919, my father was a city councilor. One day he went to Belgrade for a meeting. They brought him home in a carriage because he was suffering from shooting pains. He was admitted to the hospital, but there was nothing they could do. He died within a few hours from poisoning. He was forty-six. No medical document ever said he was poisoned, but we knew very well that the Yugoslav police eliminated him in this way for political reasons.

The Bojaxhiu family was suddenly in serious financial trouble. Nicola's business was closed down. The family was destitute. However, Drone did not lose heart. She had three children to raise: Agatha, thirteen; Lazar, eleven; and Agnes, nine. To feed her children, she courageously began a new business selling rugs, embroidery, and other products of local artisans. No one believed in the feasibility of her business but it did generate enough income to allow the family to move forward with dignity.

Meanwhile, Agnes was growing. Following her mother's example, she was a very pious girl and devoted her free time to helping the poor. At eighteen, her vocation to the religious life was openly manifested and Agnes left her family to enter the convent. She became a sister of the Congregation of Our Lady of Loreto. She first went to Ireland and then to India. From the moment she left her family, she never saw her mother or her sister again.

Mother Teresa's family continued to live in Skopje until 1934, then moved to Tirana. In 1939, Mussolini wanted to use Albania as a bridgehead to penetrate the Balkans and ordered his troops to invade the country. Lazar Bojaxhiu, who was thirty-one at the time and an officer in the Albanian army, was incorporated into the Italian army like many other Albanian soldiers. He was sent to serve in Turin, Italy. When the war ended, he decided to stay in Italy.

Meanwhile, an Albanian resistance movement was organized in Albania, which subsequently became a liberation army under the command of Enver Hoxha. When Tirana was liberated on January 11, 1946, Albania was proclaimed a people's republic and became part of the communist block. The country began a new and difficult period of intense suffering.

For forty years, Mother Teresa's homeland remained

under the dictatorship of Enver Hoxha, one of the most ruthless tyrants of the twentieth century. Enver Hoxha initially supported Stalin to reinforce his own political situation in confrontations with Albania's bordering countries. When Stalin died and Khrushchev revealed Stalin's terrible cruelty, Hoxha broke with the Kremlin and befriended Mao Ze-dong. He instituted a reign of terror within his country that was efficiently supported by a barbarous secret police force. Anyone who was suspected of disloyalty to the dictator was killed. Toward the end of the sixties, having embraced the methods of the Chinese Cultural Revolution, Hoxha eliminated forty party leaders within a few days and, in just one day, had thirty generals killed. Mother Teresa's own brother, Lazar Bojaxhiu, was found guilty of having betrayed Albania by having served in the Italian army. He was condemned to death in absentia.

Mother Teresa knew about these events and feared for her mother and sister. They were under surveillance in Tirana by the secret police because they were relatives of a condemned traitor and a Catholic nun. For ten years, she had no news from her mother and sister. Finally, a letter arrived. The two women were alive, but they were being oppressed by the regime. They had permission to write to relatives abroad only once a month and every letter had to pass through the government censor who checked every word. For this reason, Mother Teresa was never able to know the real conditions in which her mother and sister lived, nor the state of their health. From their letters she sensed they were suffering. Her mother wrote her: "I want to see you before I die. This is the only grace I ask from God."

Appealing to some important politicians she knew around the world, Mother Teresa tried every possible means to get her mother and sister out of Albania.

Toward the end of the sixties, it seemed as though her efforts were finally bearing fruit. Albania was allied at that time with China and was making some cautious efforts to open up to the West. When the French government seemed ready to initiate a dialogue, the French foreign minister, Maurice Couve de Murville, tried to help. He personally presented a request to his colleague in Tirana, but even this did not help. A while later the Albanian foreign minister wrote to Couve de Murville that "Mrs. Drone Bojaxhiu and Miss Agatha Bojaxhiu are not in a physical condition that would allow them to travel abroad." His request was refused. Mother Teresa's dream of once again embracing her mother and sister vanished. She suffered dearly. Perhaps she even wept, but she never said anything. As always, she offered her suffering to the Lord.

Drone died in 1974 at the age of eighty-three. Agatha died two years later.

Even after the death of her mother and sister, Mother Teresa continued to maintain her silence on the fate of her family. Albania was her homeland and she was waiting for the moment when she could be useful there. In fact, when Hoxha's regime collapsed, Mother Teresa and her sisters were called to work among the poor people of that nation. She responded enthusiastically and went there quickly. She did so, perhaps, in memory of her mother and sister who had contributed to the liberation of that country through their sufferings.

# FIVE

# "I DIDN'T WANT TO BECOME A NUN"

Mother Teresa first felt called to the religious life when she was twelve years old. She told me:

It's impossible to say when God calls. Perhaps a vocation is born from an intimate dialogue between God and his creature that takes place in the depths of your spirit from the first moment of life. God speaks even to the unborn, and they understand him perfectly.

As far as I can recall, I believe I felt the first strong impulse to become a missionary at around age twelve. I was going to a non-Catholic school but there were some very good priests in the parish who were zealously and diligently caring for our souls. I faithfully took part in any religious event in our parish.

One day a Jesuit missionary to India came to preach in our church. He spoke about his work in that country. His words made a deep impression on me. My heart was overwhelmed with a strong desire to go to the missions and help spread the kingdom of God. I spoke to that Jesuit about my desire and he advised me "to pray to know God's will."

For some time I continued to feel this desire to work in the missions. But at that time, I didn't want to become a nun. For that reason, my desire to go to the missions remained buried within my heart.

Thus, young Agnes Bojaxhiu did not respond affirmatively to her first small call to religious life. But she did not refuse. Agnes was not afraid of the difficulties and sacrifices that such a call presented. She did not selfishly withdraw into herself. She was perplexed because her desire to go to the missions seemed to be closely connected with choosing to become a nun.

Mother Teresa was always a practical woman, even as a child. As we have already seen, she was going through a very unpleasant period in her life at the age of twelve. Her father had been dead for three years. Her mother had to use all her energy to support her family. Agnes, even though she was still a child, had to help her and yet attend to her own needs in daily life. She had been taught to be outgoing and self-sufficient. When she felt this desire to go to India as a missionary to spread the kingdom of God, she was thinking of an active life, full of adventure, danger, and travel like the missionaries had described. She did not see how this might happen by choosing convent life.

At that time, Agnes probably did not even know what a nun's life was like since she was attending a non-Catholic school. She accompanied her mother on visits to the sick and the poor, but there was never any mention of nuns. Nuns were a rarity in Skopje since it was a predominantly Muslim city. For this reason, Agnes did not like the idea of entering the convent as a means to go to the missions.

She continued, therefore, to live in the world. But she also continued to cultivate her inner desire to help spread the kingdom of God on earth as a missionary.

The years went by, and Agnes grew. She helped her mother with the work at home, and she participated intensively in the life of the parish. "She was a beautiful girl," her brother Lazar recalls. "She was very sensitive. She loved music, played the mandolin and the piano, and wrote poetry."

In the parish the girls were part of a sodality that the Jesuits directed. Some of these priests, whom Agnes knew, went to India to work as missionaries in Bengal. However, they did not forget the friends they had left behind in Skopje and stayed in correspondence with them. One in particular, Fr. Anthony, would send one or two letters each week, giving an ample report on his and his colleagues' activities in that mission land.

These missionaries were working in the district of Noakhali, one of the most inaccessible regions of India. It comprised a group of swamps and islands scattered throughout the Ganges delta where 2.5 million people lived in an area of twenty-three square miles. The people lived miserably, crammed into squalid hovels divided by a network of canals. The only way to visit them was by boat or by a barge pulled by water buffalo.

Fr. Anthony wrote with enthusiasm and transmitted his joy and pride in being a missionary of Christ. His letters circulated among the young Catholics in Skopje, who read them avidly. Some were published in the sodality newspaper.

Agnes read these letters and was excited. They reawakened her dormant desire to serve as a missionary in India. This desire dominated her thoughts. She was no longer a child. She was almost eighteen years old, and at a point in her life when she had to seriously examine her heart and decide what she wanted to do with her life. She had to choose her own path. She felt the only thing she longed for with all her heart was to be a missionary.

She thought about it at length. She prayed. And when she was sure that she truly wanted to choose that path, she spoke about it with her mother and her parish pastor.

Her goal was to go to Bengal and work with the Jesuit missionaries there to spread God's kingdom among the people. But in order to be a missionary, she first had to become a nun. Today there are lay missionaries, but in the twenties, only nuns went to the missions. This time Agnes was more decisive. If she could not go as a lay person, she would become a nun.

Agnes wrote for information. She was told that the sisters who worked in Bengal as missionaries belonged to the Congregation of Our Lady of Loreto, whose mother-house was located in Dublin, Ireland. If Agnes wanted to go to Bengal as a missionary, she would have to apply to that motherhouse, request that she be received into the community, and then ask to be sent to India.

Agnes did not want to lose any time. She made her decision. She wrote to Ireland and after some time received an affirmative response. She left her family and went to Dublin. She entered the Congregation of Our Lady of Loreto and spent several months in Ireland, the time needed for the sisters who were responsible for new vocations to determine if this young Albanian girl had the aptitude to become a good sister within their community. In February 1929 she left for India and was sent to Darjeeling, in the Himalaya mountain region, to do her novitiate.

Darjeeling is in a marvelous location, surrounded by fantastic scenery of natural beauty. Agnes spent two years in the convent there, dedicating herself to studying the community's rule and practicing its spiritual life. After her two years of novitiate, she made her religious vows and definitively bade farewell to the world to become a bride of Christ.

The rule of the Congregation of Our Lady of Loreto, as was the custom of all religious orders at that time, required that the sisters give up their own names and take new names as a sign of their complete detachment from the world. Agnes Bojaxhiu wanted to choose the name of a French saint, St. Thérèse of Lisieux, also known as Therese of the Child Jesus. Agnes had always been fascinated by this saint, who died when she was only twenty-four years old. She had read her biography, and one thing in particular had impressed her. Even though she had always remained enclosed within the walls of her cloister, Thérèse of the Child Jesus was proclaimed the "Patron of the Missions" by the Catholic Church. Agnes was also impressed by St. Thérèse's obedience during her short life in the convent, and tried to emulate her spirit of heroic obedience. More than anything, Agnes wanted to devote herself with blind obedience, and to serve Jesus, her spouse, with total love.

Upon leaving the convent in Darjeeling, Mother Teresa was sent to a large high school that the Congregation of Our Lady of Loreto had in Entally, on the eastern edge of Calcutta. There she was assigned to get her teaching diploma because her superiors wanted her to become a teacher.

This decision was unexpected, and ran counter to her desire to be a missionary. Sister Teresa was surprised and perplexed. But reflecting on the vows that she had just made, including one of obedience, she bowed to the wishes of her superiors and prepared to leave.

# EIGHTEEN YEARS
# OF WAITING

Agnes Bojaxhiu went to India to be a missionary. She wanted to spread Christ's kingdom in that far-off land. It is for this reason she had left her mother, her brother and sister, her country, and the comfort of Western civilization. Reading Fr. Anthony's letters about his adventures among the poor in the disease-ridden swamp regions of the Ganges delta, her heart was overcome with a burning zeal. She decided to be like him and, out of love for Christ, sacrifice her own life for the poor and miserable people whom everyone had abandoned.

But Providence had other plans for her. She entered the convent, became a sister, and made her vows, always thinking about her desire to be a missionary. But instead of sending her to work among Calcutta's poor, her superiors assigned her to teach history and geography in a large high school for young Indian girls from the city's richest families.

Having scarcely begun her new profession, young Mother Teresa probably felt a little perplexed and wondered how such a change in direction could occur. Yet she immediately entrusted herself to God's will. She had just made her vows, and during her novitiate she had learned that the most important thing in spiritual life is to do God's will. Her superiors had taught her that whoever chooses to consecrate herself to God by entering the convent must sanctify herself through obedience. When she changed her name and bid farewell to the world forever, she wanted to be called Teresa and imitate the saint from Lisieux who had become a heroic example of blind obedience.

Young Mother Teresa needed only to obey. She had consecrated herself to God, and God was now her guide. God would always indicate what he wanted her to do. The perfect nun is a pliable instrument in God's hands. For this reason she had to diligently seek God's will that would mainly be manifested through her superiors. Only in this way could she be certain that she was doing his will and was carrying out the mysterious plan to which he had called her.

Mother Teresa's spirit was peaceful. Her superiors had asked her to teach high school, so she taught. She knew that this task had little to do with the missionary ideal that had compelled her to go to India. She could have been a teacher just as well in Skopje, London, Dublin, or New York, but her task was not to judge. She wanted only to obey, and so she taught history and geography for eighteen years.

In Entally the Loreto Sisters occupied a vast area where an English high school and a Bengali high school were located. Mother Teresa was assigned to the Bengali high school. Her task was to teach, but above all she was to dedicate herself to the spiritual formation of her students. These girls would become India's women—mothers, teachers, leaders, and managers—the people who would influence that country's progress. Her assignment was important yet very delicate. For this reason, she had to carry it out with the greatest of care.

Young Mother Teresa embraced her new assignment

enthusiastically. She quickly became a capable teacher. Her superiors were happy with her and appreciated her. At a certain point they appointed her principal of the school and entrusted to her direction the Daughters of St. Anne, a diocesan congregation of Indian sisters who wore a blue sari and taught in Bengal's high schools.

The years passed. Mother Teresa continued to be a history and geography teacher. But Providence, who mysteriously and attentively follows the steps of every human being, was slowly but surely preparing her for the missionary work of her dreams.

As a child she had offered herself to God to be a missionary in India. But God, who knew her and the riches of her heart, wanted much more. He wanted her to become the mother of a new and bigger mission work, the founder of an exceptional order of missionaries who were destined to bring the light of God's love to the poorest among the world's poor. It would be a difficult task that would require the highest quality of preparation. For this reason God saw to it that Mother Teresa was involved for several years behind the scenes in the extremely delicate work of the spiritual formation of young souls. And at a certain moment he also entrusted her with the direction of a congregation of sisters. In this way she gained firsthand experience for her future role as the founder of a revolutionary congregation of missionary sisters.

The high school where Mother Teresa taught was located in one of the most beautiful parts of Calcutta. It was an area that was constructed in the Western style and where the palaces of the British governor were found. Life at the high school was peaceful and comfortable. In a letter dating from that period, Mother Teresa wrote: "I teach and that is my new life. Our high school is splendid. I like teaching. I'm responsible here for an entire school and for so many girls who like me a lot."

Living at the school, Mother Teresa did not encounter the poor, homeless, destitute "untouchables" of Calcutta, those people who were dying from hunger and misery on the streets of the city. She taught in big, bright rooms, prayed in an ornately decorated chapel, took walks in a beautiful garden, and slept in a nice room on a comfortable bed protected by mosquito netting. She wore a lightweight habit and light, white shoes that enabled her to hurry through the corridors without making the slightest noise.

But all this did not touch her spirit in the least. She never forgot the missionary ideal that had set her heart on fire back in Skopje. Many biographies say that Mother Teresa was never interested in the poor while she was teaching at the high school. This is not true. The poor were always in her heart and on her mind. She did not speak about it because the Lord was calling her to do something else at that time. But she was constantly thinking about them.

At the high school in Entally there was a sodality like the one to which she belonged when she was in Skopje. The girls did various charitable and social works outside of school. At times they visited the neighboring hospital, Nilratan Sarkar, to console the sick, encourage them, and do little services like writing letters for them.

Each week a group of girls also visited the poorest areas of the city. They were genuine slums without any hygienic infrastructure and where, together with misery and moral degradation, horrible diseases were prevalent, including leprosy. Thousands and thousands of homeless people lived in those hovels, amassed like flies, forgotten by everyone, and unaccounted for even by the local government.

One of these slums, Motijhil, was behind the wall of

the school. Mother Teresa would have been able to see its wretched shacks from the school's windows. Her girls used to go to that slum. When they would return to the school, they would speak with pity and passion about what they had seen. Their stories were heartrending. Mother Teresa listened in silence. No one knows what feelings they stirred in her heart.

But one fact is certain. While teaching at the school, she never went to visit the poor who were living in the slums. She could have accompanied the students who helped out there, but she never did. Fr. Julien Henry, who was then spiritual director at the high school in Entally, has clearly confirmed this. Why did Mother Teresa never visit them, even while she was teaching at a school that was surrounded by misery?

This is a hard question to answer. But Mother Teresa certainly did not fail to visit them because she was indifferent. It could be that she had not wanted to go out among the poor because she sensed that her hour had not yet come. Or it could be that she knew she could not face so much suffering because of her sensitive heart. Or perhaps she knew herself too well, and knew if she went out just once among the poor she would never be able to let go of them and return to school to carry out her duties. That possibility was unthinkable. She had made a vow of obedience and her superiors had ordered her to teach: she had to obey.

It is possible, however, that many times secretly in her heart when she was alone at night in bed and remembered her students' heartrending stories about the indescribable suffering they had witnessed in those horrible slums, she thought about those poor people, prayed for them, and wept for them, asking God to help her find some way of alleviating their suffering. Mother Teresa knew that she was called to serve the poor, but she knew that she had to await the Lord's call. That call came decisively, like a storm, during the night of September 10, 1946.

# SEVEN

# THE NIGHT OF
# HER CONVERSION

On August 27, 1946, Mother Teresa celebrated her thirty-sixth birthday. A large party was organized at St. Mary's High School where she was teaching. Her students liked her and her birthday was an occasion for them to show her their affection and gratitude. In August, almost all the students at the school were home on vacation. But many returned specifically to honor Mother Teresa.

That year, however, her birthday was not as peaceful and joyful as the others. India was experiencing a serious political crisis. The more than four hundred million inhabitants of this large country, who were for the most part poor, were tired of the British colonial rule that had lasted for more than three centuries. They wanted their freedom and were willing to try to achieve it even if it meant bloody revolts.

At that moment events on the political scene were moving rapidly. Besides the large pacifist movement that was guided by Mohandas Karamchand Gandhi, the charismatic Mahatma who was able to fire up the crowd's enthusiasm with his doctrine of nonviolence, numerous groups of mainly Muslim fanatics took advantage of the situation and instigated riots that ended in massacres, pillaging, fires, and terrible violence.

Revolts were especially frequent in Calcutta, the most

populous city in India with the world's greatest concentration of poor people, where Hindus and Muslims were haphazardly crowded together. The latest of these revolts, the bloodiest and most frightful, had been unleashed on August 16 and had brought terror and death to the poor sections of the city. The Muslim League had declared that day a "day of direct action," inviting all of its members to demonstrate forcefully to the English and to the Hindus that the end had come.

That morning hundreds of Muslim fanatics left their shacks armed with clubs, iron bars, and shovels. Running like madmen through the streets, they unmercifully massacred every Hindu they could find, throwing the remains into the sewer ditches. They set stores and houses on fire so that within a few hours the city was covered with thick, black clouds of smoke. The police were struck with terror and went into hiding.

Caught off guard, the Hindus endured the Muslim attack. But at the first moment possible they organized themselves and counterattacked, beginning a Muslim massacre unrivaled in history. For twenty-four hours Calcutta was a battleground. Swollen cadavers floated on the surface of the Hooghly River that flowed through the city. Six thousand people were killed in one day. Then the rebels moved on to neighboring districts, to Noakhali and the province of Bihar.

The echo of the slaughters reached even the threshold of tranquility at St. Mary's High School. Mother Teresa had been following the news with trepidation, reading newspapers and listening to the stories from the school's personnel. She was horrified to learn of the torture and barbarism to which people were subjected, people who were for the most part the poorest, weakest, and most defenseless: women, children, and the elderly. Her heart was still so perturbed that on August 27, 1946, she was unable to enjoy her birthday party.

Nonetheless, the party went on as planned. Mother Teresa tried to smile as the girls brought her flowers and gifts.

While her smile was exterior and formal, a storm raged in her heart. The grave events of those days made her reflect not only on what was happening in India but also in her own life. For a while she had not been feeling at ease with herself. It seemed as though something had clogged the gears of her existence. For years everything had flowed smoothly. She had carried out her responsibilities with dedication and in a deep spirit of obedience. Now it seemed that her quiet work as a teacher in a beautiful school was no longer in tune with everything that she was experiencing within her and with the missionary spirit that she had always cultivated in her heart. "What if the Lord wants something else from me, something more having to do with the people who are suffering in this nation?" she began to wonder.

She dismissed these thoughts as temptations. She was a nun; she had made a vow of obedience and her duty was to obey.

Mother Teresa was going through a time of crisis. She did not want to admit it, but it was true. However, she was not worried. Crises are normal and happen to everyone, even those who have consecrated themselves to God. She would quickly resolve her inner doubts. In two weeks she would be leaving for a retreat where she would make some spiritual exercises. She was certain that, in that period of silence dedicated to prayer and meditation, she would be able to clarify everything.

Spiritual exercises are routine in every religious order and congregation. Their origins are found in the writings of St. Ignatius of Loyola, the founder of the Jesuits. These exercises are a sort of guide for making a general inventory of your interior life. They include meditations on death, sin, and the ultimate meaning of life, as well as practical methods of prayer and an examination of conscience. Following the example of St. Ignatius and the Jesuits, many priests and nuns make a retreat in a quiet place where they can devote themselves to a deep examination of their own spiritual lives. For St. Ignatius, the spiritual exercises lasted a month. Now they normally last a week. They are held in a place where the people can pass the time in silence, isolated from work, in order to have the closest contact possible with God through prayer.

For Mother Teresa, this year's exercises would begin on September 12. They would be held in Darjeeling, the city in Western Bengal where she had spent the two years of her novitiate. Darjeeling is located on the slopes of the Himalayas in a beautiful setting under the summit of Mount Kanchenjunga. It is a well-known resort, six thousand feet above sea level. Designed by the English, it was frequented by the wealthy population of Calcutta and is still a city for the rich, who, during the period of intense heat from May to October, take refuge there from the heat and humidity of the metropolis. During that week of spiritual exercises, Mother Teresa would also be able to rest and enjoy the cool climate of the area.

She left for Darjeeling on the evening of September 10. A railroad line linked the sprawling city on the shores of the Ganges with this Himalayan resort. Mother Teresa had decided to travel at night in order to avoid the sweltering heat that was especially intense at that time.

Arriving at the train station in Calcutta, she found herself surrounded by crowds of poor people. She knew that the city in which she had been living for sixteen years was

now the world capital of poverty. No other place on t
face of the earth had as many impoverished people as
Calcutta. But seeing them next to her as she made her
way through the station and waited for her train, it
seemed as if the situation had become worse. Along the
streets she saw horrible signs of the recent uprisings:
houses that were burned or destroyed and thousands of
people camping out in temporary shelters. There, in that
old and decaying train station, hundreds of homeless
people suffering from hunger and sickness looked like
walking skeletons. She saw young mothers begging, babies
at their breasts; groups of little children dressed in rags, following foreigners and asking for food; crippled and blind
people sitting on the ground, pointing to their mouths and
asking for something to soothe their hunger pains.

She got onto the overcrowded train. It traveled slowly,
stopping at every station. In every station there was the
same immense crowd of skeleton-like beggars.

Mother Teresa continued to examine her heart and
was terrified. She pondered. She reflected. She sought a
possible explanation for so much suffering and desolation
in her religious principles.

The filth of those poor people did not bother her. Of
course she was used to cleanliness at St. Mary's High
School. Her students were always well dressed and per-
fumed. That train, on the other hand, looked like a hospital. But her faith told her that those human ghosts who
were traveling with her or staying in the train stations
were God's children in the same way as she or her students at school. The difference was that she and her students had the good fortune of a well-to-do life while
these "children of God" were suffering immensely and
deprived of everything. Their existence was worse than
that of animals.

sa looked at the young mothers sitting on
olding their children to their breasts with
ness. The feelings of those women were no
those of rich women. Their sorrow at see-
...g     ren starving was the same sorrow an English
or American mother would experience. Mother Teresa's
heart went out to these people. She remembered the
gospel passage about the poor where Jesus said, "Whatever you do unto those little ones you do unto me." Jesus
was one of those poor people. By becoming a nun, she
had become Jesus' spouse. Thus, she had to take care of
her spouse's children by living and serving among the
poor.

Thousands of thoughts crowded Mother Teresa's mind
and heart as the train traveled on. In the heart of the night
it left the humid plains for the cool slopes of the
Himalayas. Many passengers had fallen asleep. Mother
Teresa, on the other hand, was wide awake. She felt that
something important was happening in her life.

Since she was reluctant and reticent when it came to
her own spiritual life, Mother Teresa rarely spoke about
what happened in her heart on that night of September
10. One day I asked her outright. "Mother," I said, "I
read that you felt God's call to dedicate your life to serving the poorest of the poor one night when you were
traveling from Calcutta to Darjeeling. What did you really
feel? Can you tell me about what you experienced that
night?"

Mother Teresa looked at me in silence. I thought she
would not answer, and that she would probably dismiss
the question with a few short remarks, as she generally
tended to do. However, she told me everything, and
made an extraordinary and moving confession to me.

"That night," she said, "I opened my eyes to suffering

and I understood in depth the essence of my vocation.

"I can really say that I had a new call from God that evening, a call within a call. The Lord was not inviting me to 'change' my 'status' as a sister, but to 'modify' it, so that it would be more in line with the gospel and with the missionary spirit which he gave me. It was an invitation to perfect the vocation that he had given to me when I was eighteen. I felt like the Lord was asking me to renounce my peaceful life within my religious congregation, and to go out into the streets to serve the poor. It was a clear and precise message: I needed to leave the convent and live with the poor.

"But it wasn't with just any poor people. He was calling me to serve the most miserable, the poorest of the poor in Calcutta: those who have nothing and nobody; those whom others refuse to approach because they are filthy and teeming with germs and parasites; those who can't go out and beg because they are naked, don't even have a piece of rag to put over them, and can't bear going naked in public; those who no longer eat because they are so weak from starvation that they don't have the strength to chew food; those who collapse in the street, exhausted and emaciated, conscious of the fact that they're dying; those who no longer cry because they don't have any more tears.

"These are the people that Jesus, during that trip, told me to love. I did my spiritual exercises at Darjeeling, reflecting on the message I had received. When I returned to Calcutta, I had decided to change my life."

# E I G H T

# "I HAVE DECIDED TO LEAVE THE CONVENT"

The ten days that Mother Teresa spent in Darjeeling in September 1946 were among the hardest and most important days in her life.

When she arrived, her heart was in turmoil. Drastic changes had occurred inside her during the trip. She had begun her spiritual exercises knowing that she should "revolutionize" her life. Jesus' command to her was very clear. Sister Teresa would leave the religious community that she had embraced when she was eighteen years old in order to follow her new vocation. But how would she do it?

Leaving the convent meant creating a scandal. She was a well-known and respected teacher. What would her fellow sisters, her students, and their families think? How would they look upon her?

She certainly did not want to leave the convent because she was tired of being a nun. She felt like God had called her to a new spiritual task. The Lord had shown her other ideals and other objectives that she had to fulfill. And all of this implied work outside the walls of the convent.

No Catholic religious congregation had set forth the ideals that Mother Teresa intended to carry out. The new plan she had for her life was unheard-of, highly unusual, and totally unfamiliar within traditional church organizations. Mother Teresa would have to begin a new movement, a new religious congregation, become the "foundress" of a new order.

Her ideals were grandiose and raised enormous problems, not only practically, organizationally, and financially, but also canonically and institutionally. In general, nuns who had founded new religious congregations in the course of history were nuns of a certain age who had a long history of experience in religious life and who seemed to be gifted with certain charisms. Mother Teresa was only thirty-six at the time and had been in the convent for only eighteen years. She had made her final vows in 1937, nine years before. She had been a teacher while she was in the convent, and no one had ever observed any charismatic gifts. From history's viewpoint, she did not have the necessary qualities that would enable her to obtain her superiors' immediate trust and subsequent permission to leave the convent to found a new congregation of nuns.

As a religious sister, she was under the authority of the Church and she was tied to the Church by her perpetual vows. She would not be able to do anything without the permission of her ecclesiastical superiors. To leave the convent without breaking her bonds with the Church, she would have to obtain special permission from the pope. To found a new congregation, she would need thousands of other ecclesiastical permissions. The ideals that she was determined to attain presented an incredible array of obstacles.

First of all, Mother Teresa would have to speak with her own superior at St. Mary's High School in Calcutta, and then with the superior general of the Loreto Sisters in Dublin. In the meantime, she would also have to inform the Archbishop of Calcutta because it was his responsibility to request the respective authorizations from the pope.

What arguments could young Mother Teresa use to convince these important ecclesiastical authorities to pay any attention to her? She could tell them the truth. She could tell them that one night in September when she was traveling by train from Calcutta to Darjeeling, as she looked at the poor people that were traveling with her, Jesus had "commanded" her to leave the convent and serve the poorest of the poor in the world. How would her superiors, her bishop, and the pope react to such a story?

She did not have any special prestige. Outside of those who had gone to St. Mary's High School, no one knew her. They probably would think she was some fanatic or, at the least, some young nun who no longer felt like doing her duty and was looking for a way out. They might even think her desire to serve the poorest of the poor was an excuse to escape from the difficult routine of the convent and the deadening monotony of daily obedience.

During her spiritual exercises, Mother Teresa thought about all these possibilities and weighed each one of them. She knew that what she wanted to do was extremely complicated. She realized that she would be stirring up trouble for her superiors. She suspected, moreover, that her ideas and aspirations might be from the devil. They might be temptations. She prayed intensely for some sign or confirmation. She confided in her confessor. She felt crushed by that sudden "call" that had unsettled her life.

Having finished her spiritual exercises, Mother Teresa returned to Calcutta and her work at St. Mary's High School. Preparations for the beginning of the new school year were in full swing. The girls were returning from their summer vacation. The school was coming back to life. The work of the sisters and the teachers was intensifying once again: assignments, meetings, decisions, and interviews. Work was absorbing all their time. But Mother Teresa continued to think about "her" problem.

"That 'calling' I felt the night of September 10 on the train to Darjeeling," she told me, "had all the characteristics of a command. I knew that Jesus had 'commanded' me to leave the convent. Thus, inside me I knew what I had to do. But I didn't know how to do it."

She had to move forward and begin to let people know what she was planning. She had barely begun to confide in some people when she realized how complicated the problem was.

The first people in whom Mother Teresa confided her hopes and desires were some fellow sisters who lived with her at St. Mary's High School. As she had expected, they were very perplexed and suspicious.

Then Mother Teresa spoke with the superiors of her community. They, in turn, spoke with the provincial superior, who informed the Archbishop of Calcutta, Archbishop Ferdinand Perier. As the Archbishop himself said later, the sisters were scared to death. They told him that a young sister in their community, probably too overworked, had some "strange ideas," and he had to do something before one of her whims caused a scandal.

The sisters were concerned about the reputation of their religious community and their school. They did not give due credit to their fellow sister, or adequate consideration to her spiritual problems. Indeed, they did not consider them at all. When referring the matter to the Archbishop, they took it for granted that he would arrive at the same conclusion and that he would take some disciplinary measures "against" Sister Teresa.

But Archbishop Perier was a man of great spiritual

insight. Guiding a Catholic community in a Tower of Babel like Calcutta, where religions and philosophies ranging from the esoteric to the fanatic were all mixed together in absolute confusion, was a job that required not only intelligence, astuteness, and prudence, but above all faith and great intuition. He always had to be prepared to see beyond appearances and beyond events. Archbishop Perier was accustomed to such a challenging exercise.

He had listened attentively to the provincial superior's story, but was not worried and was even less scandalized. He said only that he wanted to speak personally with the young sister and hear for himself what she wanted to do.

The meeting took place during a visit that the Archbishop made to St. Mary's High School. Archbishop Perier had a long talk with Sister Teresa, who made a very good impression on him. But he did not want her to know this. He knew that time was an important factor in shedding light on problems of the soul. Time was needed to better understand God's plan, if indeed it were God's plan.

"I told the Archbishop about my desire," Mother Teresa told me. "I told him that Jesus had asked me to leave the Congregation of the Sisters of Loreto to begin a new life helping the poorest of the poor. Archbishop Perier listened to me patiently, looked attentively into my eyes, and finally gave me a concise and precise answer: 'No.'"

No one knows what the Archbishop said to the superior of St. Mary's High School after that conversation, but he surely did not tell her to "seriously consider" Sister Teresa's desire. This only helped to further solidify the superior's conviction that her fellow sister was a victim of her own dreams and fantasies.

The difficulties were overwhelming. Now everyone in

the community knew about her plans, but no one took them seriously.

Sister Teresa encountered deep mistrust. Her fellow sisters avoided her and remained aloof from her, as though she were a traitor. They also tried to keep the students away from her, fearing that she could contaminate them with her odd ideas. She felt alone and abandoned, and suffered greatly. She sought comfort in prayer, but the thoughts, concerns, and hardships she experienced in her community had an effect not only on her mental well-being, but also on her physical well-being. She lost her appetite, began to suffer from insomnia, and complained more and more about stomach pains and migraine headaches. Her health visibly deteriorated, until she was sick.

The sisters seemed happy that she was sick. For them, it was "providential." Her illness came at the right moment to save them from a difficult and unfortunate situation. For this reason, the decision was suddenly made to transfer her to another house in the congregation.

This was a "tactical" transfer. For some time the provincial superior had wanted to get Sister Teresa away from St. Mary's High School because her "strange ideas" might have a negative effect on the girls. But she had not known what excuse to make, since everyone loved and respected her. The sister's illness was a golden opportunity and she took advantage of it.

Sister Teresa understood that it was a "punitive" transfer and thought she would never return to her teaching duties.

Archbishop Perier was not pleased with the transfer. He was looking out for the young sister, because he had seen such great faith in her eyes. When he learned that she had been transferred, he intervened so she could return to her teaching position at the high school in Calcutta. He also decided that the moment had come to take a personal interest in her case.

Mother Teresa had asked to leave the convent to begin a new mission to the poorest of the poor in the city. But she did not want her leave to be "definitive." She wanted to test how strong she was, to see if it were indeed possible to carry out the mission that she was inspired to do.

Clearly, Mother Teresa was cautious. She did not let herself get carried away by her enthusiasm. Archbishop Perier appreciated her balanced wisdom. But the political climate at that time was not favorable for such an experiment. India had just received its independence from the British. A wind of national fervor was blowing across that immense country. Inspired by Gandhi, groups of politicians and intellectuals were taking it upon themselves to do social work among the poorest people. How would they react if they discovered a European woman doing the same thing in the slums of Calcutta? Archbishop Perier told Mother Teresa to wait a while.

By this time Archbishop Perier believed in Mother Teresa's mission plan. For this reason he suggested that in the meantime she begin the canonical process to obtain permission to live outside of the convent. She immediately wrote a letter to the motherhouse in Dublin. Mother Teresa recalls:

> After a few weeks, I received an answer. Mother General was very understanding. "If the Lord is calling you," she answered, "I authorize you with all my heart to leave the congregation. Whatever happens, remember that we love you. If someday you wish to return, know that we'll always be there for you."

With Mother General's approval, I now needed

authorization from the Holy See. But the Archbishop was the one who needed to submit the request for this authorization. Archbishop Perier wasn't in a hurry. I met with him frequently, he asked me many questions, but he didn't make a decision. Finally, on February 2, 1948, he sent my request to the Sacred Congregation for Religious in Rome. Four months later, on June 1 exactly, the answer arrived. The Congregation authorized me to be a sister outside the convent. However, I had to continue to observe the rule of my congregation and obey the Archbishop of Calcutta."

Once again God's direct presence was evident in this request that was made to the higher authorities. In some mysterious way, he was guiding the footsteps of the young sister.

Sister Teresa wanted to leave the convent to work among the poor, but she wanted to do it as a religious, maintaining, so as to speak, her status as a woman consecrated to God through vows. For this reason she insisted on requesting "exclaustration," the authorization to work outside the convent. Archbishop Perier, on the other hand, wanted her to request "secularization," which would reduce her to lay status. In this way she would no longer be tied down to vows and would be completely free like any other layperson.

Writing to the Mother General, Sister Teresa asked specifically for "exclaustration." Archbishop Perier, who read the letter before approving it, had her rewrite it, requesting "secularization" instead of "exclaustration."

Reluctantly, she obeyed. She was delighted when she read Mother General's reply and saw that she understood her vocation, supported her need to work outside the convent, but suggested that she ask the Sacred

Congregation for Religious for "exclaustration" and not "secularization," just as she wanted.

Now she needed to prepare her letter to the Sacred Congregation for Religious. Availing herself of her Mother General's suggestion, she once again asked for "exclaustration." But once more the Archbishop, who was entrenched in his own ideas, rejected the letter, saying, "either ask for 'secularization' or I won't give my approval." Once again, she reluctantly obeyed. She rewrote the letter, bowing to the will of her ecclesiastical superior.

When the reply came, her heart leapt for joy. The Congregation granted her "exclaustration" and not "secularization." Thus, she could begin an experiment outside the convent, while remaining a nun bound by vows, exactly as she wanted.

This small but significant detail was yet another proof of God's will. He was the one who was guiding her destiny and she felt peaceful.

"I waited another two months to be sure about the step that I was taking," Mother Teresa told me. "On August 16, 1948, I took off the habit I wore as a sister of Our Lady of Loreto and left the convent."

# IN THE HEART OF MISERY

"Leaving the Congregation of Our Lady of Loreto was the biggest sacrifice of my life," Mother Teresa told me. "I suffered a lot when I was eighteen and left my family and country to go to the convent. But I suffered a lot more when I left the convent to begin the new experience that Jesus had proposed.

"I had received my spiritual formation, become a nun, and consecrated my life to God in the Congregation of Our Lady of Loreto. I loved the work to which the congregation had assigned me at St. Mary's High School in Calcutta. For this reason, I paid a tremendous price by taking the step of leaving forever what had become my second family. When I closed the door of the convent behind me on August 16, 1948, and found myself alone on the streets of Calcutta, I experienced a strong feeling of loss and almost of fear that was difficult to overcome."

August 16, 1948, was a Friday. On the preceding day the Church had celebrated the Feast of the Assumption, a feast commemorating one of the most disputed historical facts: the assumption into heaven, body and soul, of Mary, the mother of Jesus.

It is an ancient feast. In the Eastern Church tradition, its roots go back to the fifth century. This celebration is not just another pious belief. It is a dogma of faith, a fundamental truth in which everyone must believe in order to explain certain aspects of the reality of our existence. In

1948 it had not yet been proclaimed a dogma of faith by the pope. In fact, Pius XII would only solemnly proclaim this truth two years later, in 1950. But all Catholics knew the importance and the deep meaning of this feast.

This feast specifically exalts the ideals that Mother Teresa was striving to achieve in her new life. Mary, bodily assumed into heaven, showed us Christians the importance of our bodies. The Church teaches that our bodies are temples of the Holy Spirit, and that they will be gloriously resurrected. Jesus redeemed our bodies and souls by his passion and death. Mother Teresa was about to begin serving the poorest of the poor, people who were worth nothing, who had nothing, and whose bodies often were appalling in appearance. But even in these conditions they were still children of God. For those who have faith like Mother Teresa, Jesus was born inside those broken bodies. What Mother Teresa was about to begin was one of the greatest and most concrete testimonies of love and faith imaginable. It proclaims our splendor as human beings even in bodies that are deformed, wasted away, reduced to bones, or mutilated. Our bodies have been redeemed by Christ and will be resurrected.

Mother Teresa wanted her last day in the convent to coincide with the Feast of the Assumption as a way of giving deeper meaning to what she was about to do. She dedicated that day to prayer and meditation on the mission she was preparing to carry out, which would bring life and hope as Mary's assumption into heaven did.

Thus, Mother Teresa left the convent on the morning of August 16 for the first time in eighteen years without her religious habit. She hardly made it to the middle of the street when she was overcome by anguish. Suddenly the reality of her new state in life became clear. She was completely alone, with no house, no savings, and no work. She did not know what she would eat and where she would sleep. She found herself in that same terrible condition of those who have nothing—those whom she wanted to "serve."

She had to plan her own future. She was no longer part of a religious community, nor was she a layperson. She was still a nun, committed to God by vows of poverty, chastity, and obedience. She had only obtained the pope's permission to live temporarily outside the convent in order to found a new religious order.

She already had a very clear idea of what she wanted to do. The "command" that she received from Jesus on the night of September 10, 1946, was to "serve the poorest of the poor and to live among them and like them."

This tremendous ideal included unimaginable sacrifices. But it was an expression of total love, and it was for this ideal that Mother Teresa was making a revolutionary change in her own life.

First she had to choose a habit that would reflect her lifestyle, and that of her future companions. She chose a simple white sari, which was the most common form of dress in India, and the color most often worn by the common people. She adopted sandals as footwear.

The poor that she would be serving were mostly sick people, covered with sores and often smitten with leprosy. They urgently needed medical care. Thus, she had to learn the basic elements of medicine, such as giving injections and bandaging wounds. She needed to take a nursing course.

She moved to Patna, in the middle of the Ganges delta, where Mother Dengel and her Medical Missionary Sisters ran a hospital and offered nursing courses. She asked them to teach her nursing. "She was a good student," the sisters at Patna still remember. "She quickly learned in four months what is generally taught in a year."

After that, Mother Teresa decided to live the rule that she would later adopt for her order. She wanted to live like the poor she would be serving. The poor in Bengal ate rice and salt, so Mother Teresa tried to sustain herself for a while eating only a little rice seasoned with salt. However, such a diet did not provide enough nourishment. Mother Dengel's sisters intervened decisively. "If you continue to eat like that, you'll be committing a serious sin," they told her. "In a short time you will waste away from consumption and die. Then you won't be able to do anything for the poor. If your body doesn't have sufficient nourishment, it can't work."

Mother Teresa pondered their advice. She realized that she had been carried away by her enthusiasm and lack of experience and that her zeal could be fatal. Since these sisters had their degrees in medicine and knew what they were talking about, she realized she needed to heed their advice. So she decided that she and her future sisters would eat simply but sufficiently in order to remain in good health and totally dedicate themselves to serving the poor.

After four months, she felt that she had learned what was necessary to help the sick. She returned to Calcutta in December. Christmas was approaching and she wanted to begin working with the poor on Christmas Day. This was yet another symbolic choice that Mother Teresa made: to link her new work to one of the most puzzling mysteries of Christianity, the Nativity. Jesus, the second person of the Holy Trinity, became man, was born of a woman, and took on the form of a poor, powerless baby just like any other baby—even to the point of being born in a stable—to show that man, despite the fragility and misery of his body, is to be valued not because of his outward appearance but because he is a child of God. Thus, these poor, rejected human beings, to whom Mother Teresa was about to dedicate her life, enjoyed the same magnificent splendor as any other human being because they were children of God like everyone else.

When she arrived back in the city, she went to visit the only slum with which she was acquainted, the slum in Motijhil behind St. Mary's High School. She had heard many horrible stories about the misery in this slum, stories that had nourished her heart's generosity and contributed to help her new vocation mature. While she was living at the convent, she had never wanted to step foot in this slum. But now she decided that it would be her home.

She visited Motijhil on Christmas Day. She stopped to visit with the women and children there and searched for a place that she could fix up for her living quarters. A woman rented her a miserable shack for five rupees a month. This was her first house.

The next day, Mother Teresa's voice resounded in the shack, repeating the first letters of the Bengali alphabet. She had already found five children to teach. There was not even a table, chair, basin, or chalkboard in her room, and she used a stick to trace the letters of the alphabet on the dirt floor.

A few months before, she had been the principal of the famous high school located just a few steps away. She had taught the daughters of rich families who would in turn become teachers and professors in that marvelous school. Now she was in a slum where people lived in misery among rats and cockroaches, teaching the children of people who were nobody and who probably would never have learned to read.

The heat was suffocating in that poor shack in the middle of that miserable slum. The temperature was 115 degrees and the humidity surpassed 95 percent. Mother Teresa's clothing was clinging to her sweating body; she felt as though she was being invaded by filth. Everything was dirty: the shacks, the paths between the shacks that also served as sewer drains, the people, and the rags that people wore on their backs. On the floor of her shack, she watched insects, rats, and cockroaches running around. The children's heads were full of lice. Mother Teresa remembered her school, her nice bed, the fans that ventilated the rooms, and the clean mosquito nets. She felt as though she had passed from heaven to hell. But it was there in that hell that the poor were living, the beloved brothers and sisters of Jesus, the people whom she wanted to serve. As Mother Teresa told me:

> The change was extremely difficult. In the convent I had lived without knowing what difficulties were. I had lacked nothing. Now everything was different. I slept where I happened to be, on the ground, often in hovels infested by rats. I ate what the people I was serving ate, and only when there was a little food. But I had chosen that lifestyle in order to literally live out the gospel, especially where it says, "I was hungry and you gave me to eat, I was naked and you clothed me, I was in prison and you came to find me." Among the poorest of the poor of Calcutta, I loved Jesus. When I love like that, I don't feel suffering or fatigue.

> On the other hand, after the very beginning, I didn't have time to get bored in that slum. The five children that I had gathered on the first day of my work in the slum of Motijhil immediately increased in numbers. Three days later there were twenty-five, and by the end of the year there were forty-one. Several years later, a school was opened there that accommodates five hundred children.

Through the children, I began to penetrate those labyrinths of the most squalid misery in Calcutta. At that time, the number of homeless in the city was about one million. I went from hut to hut, trying to be useful. I helped those who slept on the sides of the street, who lived on garbage. I found the most atrocious suffering: the blind, the crippled, lepers, people with disfigured faces and deformed bodies, creatures who couldn't stand upright and who followed me on all fours asking for a little food.

One day, in a heap of rubbish, I found a woman who was half dead. Her body had been bitten by rats and by ants. I took her to a hospital, but they told me that they didn't want her because they couldn't do anything for her. I protested and said that I wouldn't leave unless they hospitalized her. They had a long meeting and they finally granted my request. That woman was saved. Afterward, when thanking me for what I had done for her, she said, "And to think that it was my son who threw me in the garbage."

On another occasion, I absolutely needed to find a hut where I could shelter some people who had been abandoned. To find one, I walked for hours and hours under the scorching sun. By evening I felt as if I were going to faint from fatigue. Only then did I understand the degree of exhaustion that poor people reach looking for a little food, a little medicine, or a roof for their heads.

"What episode from the beginning of your 'new life' do you remember the most?" I inquired.

Everything that happened then remains in my heart. There were some extremely moving experiences. I gave my life completely to God, and he was the one who guided me. I felt his presence at every moment and I saw his direct intervention.

One day, while I was walking along the streets of Calcutta, a priest came up to me, asking me to give a contribution for a collection for promoting some worthy project. That morning I had left the house with all the money I had, five rupees, which amounted to about thirty cents. During the day, I had spent four on the poor. I had only one rupee to live on the next day and the following days if something didn't happen. Trusting in God, I gave my last rupee to that priest. In my mind I prayed, "Lord, I don't have anything more, [but] I must think of you."

That evening a person whom I didn't know came to my shack. He gave me an envelope and said, "This is for your work." I was surprised because I had started my apostolate only a few days before and nobody knew me yet. I opened the envelope and found fifty rupees. At that moment I felt as though God wanted to give me a tangible sign of his approval for everything I was doing.

# T E N

# A NEW LIFE BEGINS

In the slum of Motijhil, Sister Teresa occasionally encountered some of her former students from St. Mary's High School. They, too, came to help the poor. But there was a difference. Her former students were only visiting these poor, suffering people. Afterward they returned to their homes and all their comforts. Sister Teresa, on the other hand, was living with these poor people and like these poor people. She had become one of them.

Her former students looked upon her with admiration, but also with disconcertedness. They stopped to talk with her, helped her, especially with the needs of the children, but were dumbfounded and perplexed at the choice she had made. They could not understand the reason for all her sacrifice and dedication. They felt she could have helped the poor while continuing to teach at the high school. One of them, however, was fascinated by her choice. It was clear to her that Sister Teresa was immersed in a rather heroic adventure, and such heroism always makes an impression on the souls of young people—at least in theory. In practice, their perspective changes.

Mother Teresa's own example, and the lifestyle that she would eventually choose for her future congregation, was enough to discourage anyone. She led a life of complete physical and moral sacrifice. Who could find the strength to live as she lived?

"Love that is true and great can do anything," Mother Teresa told me one day. "Only through love is it possible to face up to certain sacrifices."

For several months Mother Teresa was alone. She asked the Lord to send her company. "You commanded me to leave the convent by entrusting this new mission to me," she told Jesus. "Now it's your turn to find someone to work with me if you want me to do what you have asked me to do."

Then, at the beginning of 1949, a woman came to Mother Teresa who would become the first sister in her congregation. Shubashini Das was twenty-five years old, and had been one of Mother Teresa's students at St. Mary's High School. She came from a wealthy family. Her clothing was elegant. But she wanted to leave everything and follow Mother Teresa's example. Recalled Mother Teresa:

When she shared her desire with me, my heart throbbed. I felt great love and gratitude for her. Ever since I began my new life, I was alone. I had no one with whom I could share my plans, aspirations, and ideas. I poured out my heart to Jesus in prayer. But I really wanted to have someone nearby to talk to. I missed the companionship of the convent. When solitude is absolute, it's overwhelming. Being able to have someone with whom to live out my ideal filled me with joy.

However, I knew I shouldn't be in a hurry. I thought about how Archbishop Perier of Calcutta had been very cautious when I asked if I could change my lifestyle. For that reason, I told Shubashini Das, "Think more about it. What you're asking to do is very demanding. You might change your mind." "I've already thought about it," she insisted. I wanted to throw my arms around her and say, "Then come and live with me now." But I resisted. I thought about it for a moment and said, "Go home and pray about it. Come and see me in a few months, on the Feast of St. Joseph."

That feast day was more than two months away. I thought it would be enough time for Shubashini Das to see clearly within her. If she returned, it would mean that the Lord's call was genuine.

In the meantime, Mother Teresa continued her work in the Motijhil slum. At night she slept at the house of the Little Sisters of the Poor. A Belgian Jesuit, Fr. Celeste Van Exen, pastor of the Church of Our Lady of Sorrows, followed her activities discreetly. He had helped by finding for her a couple of rooms on the second floor of a modest house of Mother Teresa's first benefactor, Michael Gomes.

In February 1949, Mother Teresa moved into that house. She was still alone. Every once in a while a widow who cleaned at the school where she had taught would stop by and the two would spend several hours together. At the time, she was the only friend Mother Teresa had.

Mother Teresa set up her bed in the smaller of the two rooms that Michael Gomes made available to her. The larger one, which was located at the top of the stairs between the first and second floors, was transformed into a little chapel. With the help of some girls, she built a little wooden altar and hung a picture of the Immaculate Heart of Mary above it, a gift from Fr. Van Exen. Mother Teresa had prayed a lot in front of that picture during her hardest times. For that reason she wanted to hang it in the little chapel. From then on, she always took the picture with her wherever she went. Now it is in the chapel of the mother house of her congregation.

For a month, Mother Teresa lived alone in that small house. Then company came. On March 19, the Feast of St. Joseph, she got up early like she usually did. She was getting ready to go to the slum when she heard someone knock at the door. She opened it and found the fragile figure of her former student, Shubashini Das. "Mother," the young girl said, "Today is the Feast of St. Joseph and I've returned to be with you always."

She called her "mother" and not "teacher" or "sister," as was the custom at school—"mother," because having chosen to follow her in this adventure, she became her spiritual "daughter." At that very moment Shubashini Das knew she was the first of many, many "daughters."

Sister Teresa experienced great consolation in being called "mother" in this way. She, too, understood the historic importance of that moment and of the meaning of the word. She now felt that her "family" had begun its existence, the family that would be called the Congregation of the Missionaries of Charity.

Sister Teresa was no longer a simple sister. She was now responsible for another person who had placed her trust in her, like a mother. She had become Mother Teresa. Deeply touched, she threw her arms around her former student and officially welcomed her into her home.

Shubashini Das exchanged her elegant sari for a poor one like Mother Teresa wore. She also changed her name. Because of her affection for her former teacher who now had become her fellow sister, she chose the name that Mother Teresa had as a young girl, Agnes.

Mother Teresa's dream was beginning to come true. Sister Agnes was the first to join her. The following week a second girl arrived. She, too, was one of Mother Teresa's former students. Then a third came. By May, Mother Teresa had three young sisters. As she wrote to a friend: "I want to let you know that at present I have three companions who are hard workers and full of zeal. We visit five slums where we spend a few hours. There's a lot of suffering and a great need for God. Yet we are so few to bring our Lord into their midst. You should see how their faces light up when the sisters arrive. They are dirty and naked, but they have hearts full of love. I ask for your prayers. Ask Our Lady to send more sisters. Even if we had twenty more, we would have enough work for all of them in Calcutta alone."

From this letter it is clear that Mother Teresa was anxious. She needed more people for the work that she was doing with the poor. It was exhausting work, and it was not easy to find young people who were willing to make so many sacrifices.

Six months later, in November of 1949, another letter reveals that Mother Teresa now had four companions. "Pray that our little order grows," she wrote. "At present there are five of us, but, God willing, others will join us. Then we will be in a position to tie a belt of love around Calcutta and to make good use of our centers in the various slums as points from which the love of our Lord can flow out lavishly on this great city."

Mother Teresa had big plans. At that time, however, she was only thinking about Calcutta. She never imagined that one day her sisters would be spread around the world.

In the meantime some laypeople began to help her. She organized clinics in the slums where young Catholic doctors and nurses helped her take care of the sick. She was successful in getting the priest in the area to celebrate a Sunday mass for the children in the slums. "We take the children to church with their mothers," she wrote to a friend in Europe in November of 1949. "We have three hundred children and one hundred twenty mothers. Last May we had only twenty-six."

Mother Teresa's little community continued to grow. The number of young sisters grew to six, then seven, then ten. The Archbishop of Calcutta followed its development from a distance. Now that Mother Teresa already had a small group of followers, she could ask Rome for permission to officially found a new congregation. She could undertake the first step in obtaining preliminary canonical recognition. To do this, she needed to present a detailed document to Rome containing the constitution of her order and outlining its vision and rules in a clear and systematic way.

Mother Teresa began to work on it. Everything was clear in her mind because when Jesus had called her he had clearly told her what he wanted her to do. At night, while her companions were sleeping, Mother Teresa would prayerfully gather her thoughts together and write the constitution. The basic concept of her mission, to "serve the poorest of the poor," was repeated constantly, purposely, and persistently throughout.

> Our goal consists of satisfying the infinite thirst for the love of Jesus Christ by professing evangelical advice and by freely and generously serving the poorest of the poor, according to our Lord's teaching and life as expressed in the Gospel, a teaching and life that reveal God's reign in a unique way.
>
> Our particular mission consists of working for the salvation and sanctification of the poorest of the poor.
>
> As Jesus was sent by the Father, so he sends us, filled with his Spirit, to preach his Gospel of love and compassion to the poorest of the poor around the world.
>
> Our major concern should be to proclaim Jesus Christ to men and women of all nations, especially those who are entrusted to our care.

We are called the Missionaries of Charity.

"God is love." The Missionary of Charity must be a missionary of love, full of charity in her soul, and spread it to the souls of others, both Christian and non-Christian.

From her religious order's constitution and rules, it is clear that the mission Mother Teresa entrusted to her congregation was very evangelical, based on that fundamental teaching of Christ, which is love. But it was also ecumenical in scope and embraced all of mankind, "Christian and non-Christian," because Christ's saving love is universal.

Love, as expressed through the gospel word of "charity," was a distinctive element of the new order. At first, Mother Teresa wanted to make this concept more explicit and call the sisters "Bearers of Christ's Love to the Slums." But she opted for "Missionaries of Charity" since it is more concise and less restrictive. In order to "live out" this concept of love with utmost intensity, Mother Teresa wanted her sisters to take a special vow when making their profession. In addition to the three traditional vows of poverty, chastity, and obedience common to all religious orders, she wanted her sisters to be united to God with a vow of "charity." As Mother Teresa explained to me, "We make a commitment with this vow to freely and devotedly serve all the underprivileged. This vow means that we cannot work for the rich and that we cannot accept any recompense for the work we are doing."

As to the religious habit of her congregation, Mother Teresa decided to adopt the Indian sari that she and her coworkers were already wearing, a white sari made from coarse fabric with a border of three sky blue stripes. The sari is fastened on the left shoulder with a clasp in the form of a crucifix to remind the sisters of the cross that

Jesus carried. "The sari," Mother Teresa told me, "helps the sisters... identify with the sick, with children, and with abandoned old people by sharing the same clothing and the same lifestyle as the underprivileged people of this world."

Mother Teresa presented her constitution to the Archbishop of Calcutta, who examined it carefully, had his experts look it over, and then sent it to Rome. On October 7, 1950, Vatican approval arrived. From then on the congregation was officially recognized. As Mother Teresa recounted:

That October 7 was a great day for us, the official canonical beginning of our congregation. I was happy that the document from Rome arrived on October 7, which is the Feast of Our Lady of the Rosary. The coincidence seemed to be a sign from heaven. Archbishop Perier came to celebrate mass in our little chapel and Fr. Celeste Van Exen read the bull [papal decree] from Rome during the ceremony.

From that moment, our congregation continued to grow. I opened three other houses, all in the Archdiocese of Calcutta, since canon law stipulates that a new religious institute cannot expand beyond the diocese where it originated for a period of ten years. But when this period was barely over, we began to open houses in other cities in India as well.

When a congregation receives authorization from the Sacred Congregation for Religious and the approval of the bishop of the diocese where it began, it becomes a diocesan order. It has attained the first important step for its growth. As it grows larger, it can be approved by the Pope with the *Decretum Laudis*. In general it is necessary to wait several decades for such pontifical approval. But the Lord was good to us even with this. We waited for pontifical approval only fifteen years. On February 1, 1965, Pope Paul VI gave pontifical approval to our congregation, and in that same year we opened our first house outside of India, in Cocorote in the Diocese of Barquisimeto, Venezuela.

# E L E V E N

# TESTIMONIES OF LOVE

When Mother Teresa was telling me about the beginnings of her congregation, we were at the house of the Missionaries of Charity at Casilina in Rome.

We talked under a shade tree in the garden where Bishop Paul Hnilica, the Slovak bishop who introduced me to Mother Teresa, was seated next to her. Mother Teresa was deeply engaged in our conversation. Although she was very discreet when talking about her own personal life, she was very communicative when the conversation focused on her sisters or the work they were doing.

It was a delight to be there under the blue sky, listening to her. The mild temperatures of Rome in May and the green that was bursting forth as spring unfolded contributed to an atmosphere of peacefulness and optimism. Time passed quickly. Without warning, Mother Teresa remembered that she had to do something and asked what time it was.

"Eleven o'clock," I answered after checking my watch.

"I have to go to the Vatican. I'm late," Mother Teresa said, standing up. "We'll continue our conversation tomorrow. Tomorrow morning fourteen of my sisters will be making their vows at St. Polycarp's Church. Please come. It would give me great pleasure if you could attend that ceremony. Afterward we can talk some more."

Bishop Hnilica offered to accompany Mother Teresa to the Vatican in his car. "Gladly," she answered with a smile.

She sat in the backseat and I had the privilege of sitting next to her. Bishop Hnilica sat next to the driver, Fr. Labo, a Slovak priest and a skillful driver who was capable of navigating Rome's chaotic traffic with incredible safety. "With him," Bishop Hnilica noted, "we'll make up for the lost time and arrive at the Vatican on time."

We drove off quickly. Mother Teresa asked us to join her in prayer. She made the sign of the cross and took a rosary out of the pocket of her sari and began to pray. She prayed slowly and softly as we responded.

Our car darted through the traffic. At times it stopped abruptly, swerved suddenly, took off quickly, and turned corners recklessly, barely missing other anxious and aggressive drivers who hurled threats or blew their horns, hoping to pass us. I grabbed on to my seat belt and looked anxiously at our brave but foolhardy driver. Mother Teresa, on the other hand, was absorbed in prayer and oblivious to everything. Huddled in her seat, she was united with God in prayer. Her eyes were partially closed. Her wrinkled face was transformed by a look of ecstasy and serenity. She prayed the words of the prayers with an enchanting tenderness and truly seemed to be conversing with an invisible presence. She gave off a mysterious charm that produced an aura of silence and reverence.

When the rosary was finished, Bishop Hnilica began to point out various Roman monuments along the road to me. Mother Teresa, on the other hand, continued her conversation with the invisible presence in silence. She always had her head bowed down and her eyes closed. Her lips moved slightly. It was only when we were approaching St. Peter's Square an hour later that she "returned to our midst" and started to talk with us in her usual polite way.

We stopped at the entrance to the Vatican where the

Swiss Guards are stationed and got out of the car. Bishop Hnilica told us to wait and went to a telephone. Some girls recognized Mother Teresa and ran up to her, shouting, "Mother Teresa, Mother Teresa!" They kissed her hand and asked for her autograph. She greeted them and then withdrew humbly and timidly into a corner. She did not like being the object of so much attention.

She walked up to me. "Tomorrow at St. Polycarp's Church, outside of Rome," she reminded me. "It's a very moving ceremony. Remember, I'll be waiting for you."

"I'll definitely be there," I answered.

At that moment Bishop Hnilica returned. "Let's go," he said to Mother Teresa. "The pope is waiting for you."

I said goodbye to Mother Teresa and returned to my hotel.

The next morning I arrived at St. Polycarp's Church at eleven o'clock sharp. The church was already filled with people. Everyone's eyes were fixed on the main entrance because they wanted to see Mother Teresa. When she entered, surrounded by the young sisters who were going to make their vows, people began to applaud. Many were crying.

Without looking up, Mother Teresa continued to walk with her sisters. She walked across the church, approached the altar, and knelt down in a corner.

The ceremony truly was moving. The celebrant gave a long sermon. Mother Teresa also spoke, but briefly. Among other things she said: "Our work is hard. We are serving the poor and the homeless twenty-four hours a day. We don't refuse to help anyone. Young people who ask to enter this congregation know that they are going to encounter difficulties, but face them with a spirit of generosity because their hearts are full of love."

People followed the ceremony attentively. In Rome,

everyone loves and holds in high regard the Missionaries of Charity. They affectionately refer to them as "the Indian sisters."

Many other Missionaries of Charity were scattered throughout the crowd as they watched their fellow sisters make their vows. Looking around, I counted about fifty, all wearing white saris with blue borders like Mother Teresa. The work they do in their four houses in Rome is exhausting. They have a special interest in those people who have been neglected or abandoned by other religious orders and humanitarian organizations. Every night they try to bring a word of comfort and hope to people in the area around Rome's main train station, the Stazione Termini, which is populated by drug addicts, transvestites, prostitutes, street people, and thieves. Even the police are afraid of patrolling that area at night. Nevertheless, Mother Teresa's "Indian sisters," armed with great love, venture there.

I walked around the church and attentively observed the sisters as they knelt in the pews among the people. Reflecting on the hard life they had embraced, I experienced at the same time a sense of admiration and a feeling of dismay. They were all young; some were *very* young. Their faces, though smiling, had that severe look to them that is characteristic of those people who always have a lot on their minds. Their rough, chapped hands showed that they were painfully accustomed to exhausting labor.

When the ceremony was over, I went to see Mother Teresa. She was happy to see me and to know that I made it to the ceremony. Since her day was already full and she could not find any other time to talk to me, she asked me to join her in the car that was taking her to the mother-house at San Gregorio al Celio so that I could ask her more questions en route.

Allegri: *Before making their vows, what kind of training do your sisters have?*

Mother Teresa: When a girl enters our congregation, she observes us for a period of time. She sees how we live and asks herself if she really wants to make our life her life. Once she has made that decision, she begins her novitiate, which lasts for two years. During that time, the young sister concretely learns about the work she'll always be performing by doing it together with other sisters who have already made their vows. Later she will assist the dying, help the poor, and ask for alms for those who have nothing. In short, she'll do all the tasks that we carry out in general, putting herself in a position where she will experience in a practical way the life that she wishes to choose. If she can withstand it, she will make her profession of vows after two years, committing herself before God and the Church to seek sanctity according to the rule of our congregation.

Allegri: *What's a typical day for the sisters?*

Mother Teresa: Above all, it consists of prayer. Contrary to what people think, we are not sisters who are engaged in an active life. We are contemplative sisters who live in the world. Prayer, then, is fundamental for us. We always pray, whether it be walking down the street, during our work, or wherever. If we're not continually united with God, it would be impossible to make the sacrifices that are required for living among those who have been forsaken.

Allegri: *What time do you get up in the morning?*

Mother Teresa: At four thirty. We spend an hour and a half in prayer together, have breakfast, and then leave for work. Each sister's work is determined by the needs of the place where she is working. Here in Rome, for example, my sisters help people who are sick and lonely. They help old people who are unable to look out for themselves by cleaning their homes, doing their laundry, and keeping them company. Often they go begging in order to feed those who don't have anything.

Allegri: *What time do you go to bed in the evening?*

Mother Teresa: In general, at ten o'clock. But if necessary, we also work all night.

Allegri: *Are these hours normal for all your houses, or are they modified depending on the place where the sisters are working?*

Mother Teresa: They're normal for all our houses, but we're not inflexible. Rules must serve our mission, which is the welfare of those we're helping. Love is above everything, even if love must be governed by a strict discipline.

Allegri: *Do you also keep these hours?*

Mother Teresa: Yes, I'm a sister just like the others.

Allegri: *Don't you find it difficult at your age to get up at four thirty in the morning?*

Mother Teresa: Even for my youngest sisters it's difficult to get up at that time. But sacrifice is a way of showing love for Jesus, and my heart is young.

Allegri: *Recently you were quite ill and had a heart operation.*

Mother Teresa: I'm in God's hands. I work for him. I don't have time to ask myself how I'm feeling. *He'll* tell me when it's time to stop.

Allegri: *How many sisters are there in your congregation at this time?*

Mother Teresa: Three thousand. They live in 303 houses in 75 countries. We've received 140 requests to open houses, but it's impossible to respond to all of them. We would need many more vocations than the Lord has already sent to us.

Allegri: *When the communist countries were still strict dictatorships, avowedly atheistic and therefore hostile to religion, you obtained permission to open houses even in those coun-tries. How did you do it?*

Mother Teresa: Works of love are works of peace. We've never been interested in politics, and everyone wishes us well. The Missionaries of Charity began working in various communist countries like Poland, Yugoslavia, East Germany, and the Soviet Union before the communist ideology experienced a crisis. We went to those countries because there were poor people even there who needed our love.

Allegri: *You are Catholic sisters. You help the poor, but aren't you also spreading the Catholic religion?*

Mother Teresa: If someone possesses a treasure, it's only fair to share it with others. However, we never take the initiative. We don't proselytize.... We love everyone in a concrete way out of love of God. Our works reveal to the poor who are suffering the love that God has for them.

The results are always marvelous. One day in India, an American journalist was watching me while I was caring for a man with gangrene. The journalist told me, "I wouldn't do that for a million dollars." "Even I wouldn't do it for that amount," I answered. "However, I do it out of love for God. This poor, suffering man represents the body of Christ for me." That journalist was struck by my words, and grasped what is the force that sustains our work.

Here in Rome, something very significant happened. While going around looking for people who had been abandoned, some of our sisters came across an old atheist. He was a prisoner of his suffering and loneliness. He was turned in on himself and didn't say even a word to the sisters who found him. But they didn't give up. They washed his linens, cleaned his house, and prepared a little food for him. Still he wouldn't speak. Then the sisters decided to visit him twice a day. Finally, after a week, he was won over by all their affection and broke his silence. He said, "Sisters, you have brought God into my life. Now bring me a priest so I can go to confession. I haven't done so for more than sixty years." The love of those sisters got that man to think and brought about his conversion. They hadn't spoken to him about God, but he understood that the way they related to him could only have been inspired by God.

Some sisters met an alcoholic in Melbourne, Australia. He had been an alcoholic for many years and had lost all dignity. He lived like an animal. The sisters took him into our House of Mercy, washed him, gave him some decent clothing, and helped him get detoxified. After a few weeks he was a new man and was able to return home. He began to work again. When he received his first paycheck, he brought it to us and said: "I want you to be the love of God for others like you were for me."

These are some little examples that show how it's not necessary to speak about God in order to convert people. It's enough to witness by the way you live.

Allegri: *What are the main ways in which you work?*

Mother Teresa: We try to be present where there is suffering that has no hope and where the poor and the sick have been abandoned by everyone. We haven't planned out our work. We've developed it little by little as the needs presented themselves. God has always been the one to show us what we should do.

At first I began by teaching the poorest children in the slums of Calcutta. Then I organized clinics for distributing medicine to the sick and food to the hungry. I organized professional schools in order to teach the poor how to earn their living. Then I saw many other ways of being present where suffering calls for our help.

The car turned left, passed by the Colosseum, and climbed up a small street toward the beautiful church of San Gregorio al Celio, where the motherhouse of the Missionaries of Charity is presently located in Italy. Several people were already waiting for Mother Teresa. I said goodbye to her. "Come again tomorrow morning," she said. "Mass is at five. You can enter through that little door, which is always open at that time."

# TWELVE

# "HERE'S MY BUSINESS CARD"

I slept very little that night. I kept thinking about my conversations with Mother Teresa. Thanks to Bishop Hnilica, who had introduced me to her as a friend and continued to help me speak with her at length, my meetings with her were very fruitful and provided me with some extremely interesting material. Between our meetings I was already in the process of organizing it. At night, I would reflect over and over again on what she had told me.

That morning at four o'clock I leapt out of bed at the sound of the alarm, feeling full of energy. Within a half hour I was in the lobby, waiting for my taxi.

Rome has an arcane charm to it at that hour. Its streets are deserted. Its palaces and monuments, enveloped in that mysterious darkness preceding dawn, seem like living beings that are holding their breath while they wait for the big event to occur.

My taxi sped along. Some windows were lit up. A stray dog crossed the street.

Since I was early, I told the taxi driver to stop in front of the Colosseum. From there I walked to the Church of San Gregorio al Celio.

The little door on the side of the church that Mother Teresa had pointed out to me the day before was open. I went in. I knew where the chapel was from a light that was coming from some windows. I approached the chapel and looked through the windows. Some sisters were already kneeling inside. I took a seat in a corner at the back so I would not disturb anyone.

The sisters continued entering the chapel from their small rooms where they had rested during the night. Mother Teresa also arrived and knelt down on the stone floor like the other sisters. She had no specially reserved seat, even though she was the "founder," the mother superior and mother general of her congregation. In all the other religious institutes, the mother superior is revered, served, and treated in a special way. But Mother Teresa of Calcutta never wanted any special privileges. She always wanted to be considered equal to her fellow sisters, equal even to the newly arrived postulants and novices. That morning, too, she was with the other sisters in the back of the chapel.

From my seat I could see her well and I watched her closely throughout mass. I knew that I should not have been distracted during the liturgy and that I should have been praying like the sisters, but I was sure that the Lord would understand. Besides, the admiration that was stirred up in me when I saw the concentration, humility, and gentleness on Mother Teresa's face while she conversed with God was also a form of prayer.

As the celebrant left the altar after the liturgy, a sister came up to me and signaled me to follow her. She took me to a little room and told me to wait there because Mother Teresa would arrive shortly.

After about ten minutes, Mother Teresa came in. She was carrying a tray with breakfast: coffee, milk, jam, rolls, and fruit. I wanted to do something to stop her from going through such trouble, but I was unable to do so.

She had me sit down at a little table in the middle of the room and wanted to serve me. I protested out of embarrassment, but Mother Teresa smiled lovingly. She asked me if I wanted honey instead of sugar to sweeten my coffee. Then she explained that she was late with breakfast because she wanted to say goodbye to those sisters who would be leaving to work in the city. "It's a beautiful day," she said. "Today they won't be bothered much by the heat."

She was at ease as she spoke. She asked me whether I liked the ceremony I attended the previous day where the sisters made their vows. "Very much so," I answered.

"You should come and see us in Calcutta," Mother Teresa said. "There you could breathe the real air of our congregation and understand the deep meaning of the work that Jesus wants us to do."

"I would very much like to go to Calcutta," I answered. "I should try to come as soon as possible. Give me your address and telephone number. I'll write them down and try to visit you."

Mother Teresa took my note pad, opened it, and wrote down her address. Then she told me with a smile:

One day, I met a very rich and important person in America. He gave me his business card and asked me for mine. "I don't have a business card," I answered. "What?" he said, amazed. "A famous and important woman like you should have a business card. Here in America people of importance are very attentive to this custom. I recommend that you get some business cards as soon as possible, and you'll see how useful they'll be."

I listened to what that man had to say. I, too, had some business cards printed. But I didn't have my titles and credentials printed on them as is the custom because I am nothing, less than nothing. I had some things printed on them that are my plan in life.

Mother Teresa searched in the pockets of her sari and gave me one of those cards. It was a rectangle of cheap, faded, bluish paper. On it was written:

> JESUS is happy to come with us,
> as the TRUTH to be told,
> as the LIFE to be lived,
> as the LIGHT to be lit,
> as the LOVE to be loved,
> as the JOY to be given,
> as the PEACE to be spread.
>
> Mother Teresa

On the right side of the card there was a drawing of two hands joined in prayer. "This card," Mother Teresa said, "enables me to do what is customary among the important people I often meet. They give me their business cards and I give them mine. At the same time I'm spreading a good thought, a message. Maybe someone reading these lines will reflect on their importance. Even that would be good."

"You seem rested," I said. "Yesterday I thought you looked very tired."

"I had a good rest," Mother Teresa said.

"During these last few years you've had some rather delicate operations, like the one on your heart. You should take care of yourself and travel less."

"Everyone tells me that. But I have to think about the work Jesus has given me. When I shouldn't be serving any more, he'll be the one to stop me."

"Are you afraid of dying?" I asked.

My question caught Mother Teresa off guard. She looked into my eyes for a few moments. Perhaps she was not expecting such a question. Then she asked me, "Where do you live?"

"In Milan," I answered.

"When are you returning home?"

"I hope to return this evening," I said. "I'd like to catch the last plane out so I can be at home with my family since tomorrow's Saturday."

"I see that you're happy to go home and to be with your family," she observed.

"I've been gone for almost a week," I said, trying to justify my enthusiasm.

"That's fine," she added. "It's all right for you to be happy. You're going back to your wife, your children, your loved ones, your home. It's all right for it to be like that."

She was silent for a moment, and then continued: "Well, you see, I would be as happy as you are if I could say that I was going to die this evening. By dying, I, too, would go home. I would go to see Jesus. I consecrated my life to Jesus. By becoming a sister, I became Jesus' spouse. You see, I have a wedding band on my finger just like married women do. I'm married to Jesus. Everything that I'm doing here on earth, I'm doing out of love for him. Therefore, when I die, I will be returning home to be near my spouse. Furthermore, up there in heaven, I'll see all my loved ones. Thousands of people have died in my arms. I've spent more than forty years of my life caring for the sick and the outcast. My sisters and I have picked up thousands and thousands of dying people from the streets, especially in India. We've taken them to our homes and we've helped them to die in peace. Many of these people died in my arms while I smiled and caressed their trembling faces. Well, when I die, I'm going to see all these people again. They're there waiting for me. We loved each other in those difficult moments. We've continued to love each other in our memories. Maybe they'll have a party for me when they see me. How can I be afraid of death? I desire it and wait for it because I'll finally be able to go home."

I never heard Mother Teresa talk at such length and with such enthusiasm. In general she was very concise when being interviewed, and her responses were brief and quick.

On that occasion, she responded to my rather strange question with a bona fide speech. While she spoke, her eyes sparkled with amazing peace and happiness.

In the meantime, I had finished breakfast. Mother Teresa put the cups back on the tray and folded the tablecloth that she had spread out. A young sister appeared at the door and Mother Teresa handed her the tray. "Now we can take up our conversation that was interrupted in Casilina the other day," she said.

# T H I R T E E N

# THE HOME FOR
# THE DYING

My first meeting with Mother Teresa took place in the house of the Missionaries of Charity in Casilina. That morning Mother Teresa recalled how her mission began. She spoke to me about the work she had done in the Motijhil slum, the arrival of her first sisters, and the joy she experienced when she was granted pontifical authorization by Rome to begin a new religious congregation. Her story stopped in 1953.

Later I met her at Tor Fiscale and accompanied her by car to San Gregorio al Celio, but our conversation during these meetings focused on particular aspects of her work.

Finally, that morning in San Gregorio al Celio, Mother Teresa had some free time. I was able to talk to her in a somewhat relaxed way. In that little room in the convent, Mother Teresa resumed her story, from the moment when she had to leave Michael Gomes' house because it had become too small for her and her sisters.

"There were already thirty of us," she smiled happily. "We simply had to leave that house."

But it was not easy to find a new living situation. Mother Teresa did not have any savings or political connections. Her friends were merely beggars. She entrusted the matter to prayer. Every evening for three months she and her sisters walked in procession to the statue of our

Lady of Fatima that Fr. Julien Henry had set up near his parish. After working all day long, they would leave at around six o'clock and walk down the street to the statue as they recited the rosary aloud. It was quite a distance from their house, and along the way many people would join them. They returned around nine o'clock, still praying. "We literally assaulted heaven with our prayers to obtain a new residence," Mother Teresa told me. "And heaven heard us."

A house with three floors that was part of a small complex had become available. It was adequate for the congregation, but Mother Teresa did not have any money to buy it. Archbishop Perier of Calcutta intervened and paid the amount needed, thereby showing his esteem for the Missionaries of Charity. Thus, the sisters were able to move to their new headquarters, which continues to serve as the motherhouse for the congregation to this day.

During this period, Mother Teresa began one of her most brilliant and extraordinary charitable works: the Home for the Dying.

Calcutta is one of the most populous cities in India. From the moment India was given its independence, thousands of refugees arrived in the city, looking in vain for housing. Victims of hunger and disease roamed around the city, especially on the outskirts. Every day dozens of these poor, homeless people collapsed on the ground from lack of strength. Many died on the street.

The government hospitals and clinics tried to help these people but, given the large number of cases that only grew day by day, they were able to do very little. They tried to help those who could be saved, but abandoned the old and very sick to their fate since they would only die if they were admitted to the hospital.

These unfortunate people, therefore, were at the mercy

of their sad fate. When their strength was no longer sufficient to sustain them, they collapsed on the ground until they were dragged to the side of the road to die, as other people passed by totally unconcerned. As Mother Teresa recounted:

One day while I was leaving our house, I came across a man lying on the sidewalk who was on the brink of death. I was at Campbell Hospital. I went to get help at a nearby hospital but they refused to admit him because they didn't have any room and the man would die anyway. I was upset by their response. For me, that man was a son of God and I couldn't leave him in the middle of the street in his condition. I went to a pharmacy for some medicine but when I returned after a few minutes he was already dead. He breathed his last breath in the dust on the street.

It was a shame. I almost felt guilty. I told myself that I needed to do something. Then the idea occurred to me of creating a home where these dying people could finish out their lives, where someone would help them, where they would see the face of a person next to them who would smile lovingly and help them understand they shouldn't be afraid because they were going to their Father's house.

My fellow sisters completely supported my idea. But we had to find a building for these dying people.

I went to the city administrator and then to the director of sanitation. "Give me at least a room," I asked. Everyone praised my idea. Various solutions were considered. However, I didn't have the money or the means to resolve the problem alone. Finally, they thought about giving me permission to use, at least temporarily, a rest house for pilgrims that was annexed to the temple of the goddess Kali, which had been vacant for a while. I called that house *Nirmal Hriday,* which means "The Place of the Immaculate Heart" in Bengali.

We began our work at once. Nevertheless, there was a lot of opposition. The house was set up on the holy site of the popular Temple of Kalighat with its four hundred priests. Someone was saying that my sisters and I were going there to convert the people to Christianity. There were attacks and lawsuits. Many people sided against us, while others supported us.

An Indian political leader made a promise in public that we would be thrown out, whatever the cost. He came to see us while collecting complaints against us. He walked down the passages between the dying and observed our sisters at work. He was touched by what he saw. He saw that they were devoting themselves to those unfortunate people with great love, cleaning the wounds of their feeble bodies, and feeding those who could not feed themselves. When he left, he told the people who were waiting for him: "I promised to throw the sisters out of here and I'll do it, but only when you bring your mothers, wives, sisters, and daughters to do the work that they are doing. You have a goddess of stone in the temple; here you have living goddesses."

Shortly thereafter, one of the priests of the goddess Kali came down with tuberculosis, a disease that is still highly feared in India. We took in that priest and kindly took care of him. Every day one of his fellow priests would visit him, and each one went away very impressed by our care for this priest and the other sick people. One by one, all the priests of the goddess Kali became our friends and supporters. The hostility ended and we were able to continue our work in peace.

The Home for the Dying is something dear to my heart. It has become a holy place because there every day I see actual contact between heaven and earth: indeed, many people close the door on their earthly experience to unite themselves to the Father. You can concretely feel the presence of God by helping these people.

When we rescue the dying, they are scared, distressed, and in despair. But seeing our calm and serene faces bending over them with tenderness and love and listening to our words of faith and hope, they close the door on their lives with a smile on their lips.

One day the sisters picked up a man on the street whose body was covered with sores and full of worms. He was at the end of his life. I began to wash him and care for him. With his dying eyes, he followed every movement I made. Little by little, a peacefulness appeared on his face. "Are you suffering?" I asked him. "A lot," he answered in a whisper. Then he added: "But I'm happy. I've always lived in the open, like the animals. Now I'll die like an angel, surrounded by so much care and so much love."

Another time, they brought home a woman who no longer had any human resemblance and who didn't show any sign of life. I washed her, took care of her, and talked to her gently. Then I carefully set her down on a bed. She took my hand and smiled. I've never seen such a beautiful smile on anyone's face. "Thank you," she whispered and closed her eyes forever.

During his visit to India, even John Paul II came to visit the Home for the Dying. He spent a long time there. He wanted to feed some old people and was present for the death of three people. During all the time he was there, he wasn't able to say a word. He was deeply moved and warm tears fell from his eyes.

Allegri: *How many people have died in your arms in the Home for the Dying?*

Mother Teresa: I don't know. Thousands. At this point, we've cared for about 50,000 people in the Home for the Dying, of which more than half have died.

Allegri: *After having seen so many people breathe their last breath, have you become accustomed to death?*

Mother Teresa: It's impossible to remain indifferent to death when you know that it's the most important moment in a person's life. Every time someone dies in my arms, it's as if I've seen Jesus die. I help him with the love I have for God.

The Home for the Dying has become a holy place. Mother Teresa considered it her most precious work ever. "God is here," she always said when talking about the home.

The low, whitewashed building is always open. It doesn't really have any doors. Anyone can come in, and often young men and women join the sisters, helping those who have been brought in to die with a smile on their lips.

The dying come in ambulances, cars, and hand-drawn carts. The sisters wash them, treat them, and care for them. The cots are arranged in three rows in a soft light.

A statue of the Virgin Mary is in one corner. She has a crown on her head made from the gold rings that women who have died in that place used to wear in their noses.

Mother Teresa was the one who had the idea for the crown. She had it made and then, putting it on the Virgin's head, said: "Those who had nothing on earth have given a gold crown to the Mother of God." The statue has a big ribbon with the Padmashree Medal attached to it, a prestigious award that the Indian government gave to Mother Teresa in 1962.

In 1973 an Indian chemical company gave Mother Teresa a large, new building as a gift, a building that was going to be used to house the company's laboratories. Many people thought that Mother Teresa would move the dying to that building, but she didn't. "I'll never leave Kalighat," she said. She called the new building *Prem Dan,* which means "gift of love." She set it aside for those people who have a good chance of surviving. Prem Dan is a sort of hospital where the needy come to recover, even if it is for a long period of time. They are released when they are able to walk on their own feet and have a way of supporting themselves.

## F O U R T E E N

# "I'M THE MOTHER OF THOUSANDS OF CHILDREN"

There are thousands of photographs of Mother Teresa. Even though she was very shy and rather averse to having her picture taken, she was one of the most photographed people in the world during her lifetime. Her popularity was so great that, whenever she appeared in public, camera lenses were focused on her. Newspapers, magazines, and television stations frequently sent reporters to Calcutta to do reports on Mother Teresa. She never shirked from these requests. She knew that her pictures served to draw the world's attention to the problems to which she had devoted her life.

The dramatic pictures of Mother Teresa walking around Calcutta among the lepers, the crowds of abandoned people in the slums, the poor people in their crumbling shanties, and the dying were published regularly. In general, Mother Teresa's wrinkled face looks sad, tired, and preoccupied in these pictures.

On the other hand, she appears a totally different person in those photos where she appears with children. In those photos, she appears peaceful and relaxed. Her eyes shine with love. It is evident that she was overcome with an intense, maternal love that deeply touched her.

Nonetheless, Mother Teresa rarely smiled, even with a

child in her arms, because the children that she held were always children who had been abandoned—orphans, lepers, victims of ethnic violence—and whose eyes had been filled with frightening images. By holding them in her arms, Mother Teresa hoped that they would feel an intense love that would stem their suffering and fear. As Mother Teresa said to me:

> Children are the most beautiful gift that God can give us. But man, because of his selfishness, doesn't always appreciate this gift. Often children are rejected, abandoned, and even murdered. I've always fought against these crimes. I do everything I can to draw attention to this problem.
>
> Children have played an important part in my life and my work. After leaving the Convent of Our Lady of Loreto, I began my new mission with five little children. They lived in the slum of Motijhil on the outskirts of Calcutta in the most wretched part of the city. I had nothing, but I looked for food in the garbage for them. We were together. I loved them and they were happy. There is no greater sadness in the world than an absence of love. I have seen children left to die because no one cares about them.
>
> The plight of children who have been abandoned is difficult to understand. Animals rarely abandon their offspring. Man, on the other hand, does. This crime is just as prevalent in rich countries as in poor ones. It occurred in the past when people were considered less civilized, and it continues to occur even today on the threshold of the third millennium.

This problem is more acute in India than in other countries. The extreme poverty that afflicts a large part of the population has a disintegrating effect on nuclear families. Rampant diseases contribute to the birth of handicapped children, who are subsequently rejected by their parents. A widespread "macho mentality" fosters a disinterest in newborn girls. In India, it is easy to find newborn infants who have been abandoned inside churches, in front of hospitals, on the steps of convents, outside police stations, or simply thrown in the gutter. This was especially true in Calcutta after the war, when the city was going through one of the most difficult times in its history.

Abandoned children are truly the poorest and most defenseless creatures on earth. Religious institutes have always tried to help these children. Many congregations of sisters have been founded for the specific purpose of caring for orphans and children who had been rejected by their parents. Mother Teresa's missionaries have also included helping abandoned children in their many charitable activities.

As we have seen, Mother Teresa began her new mission on Christmas Day in 1948 by caring for some children living in the slum of Motijhil. They were not really "abandoned" children, in the true sense of the term, because they did have families, albeit families afflicted by enormous problems of poverty and disease. However, their families took no interest in them and they were left to fend for themselves, roaming around and spending their time begging. Mother Teresa got these children off the street by gathering them in a hut. She then taught them the alphabet and basic rules of hygiene that would help them to avoid diseases.

But Mother Teresa's enormous heart could not remain indifferent to the call of those newborn babies who were rejected by their parents and had no one else in the world. In 1954 Mother Teresa founded her first home for abandoned children. She called it *Shishu Bhavan*, which means

"Children's Home." People began to bring to her new-born babies found abandoned in the city and soon the house was too small to meet the need. Mother Teresa had to open another *Shishu Bhavan* and then others, as she explained to me:

I'm the mother of thousands of abandoned children. I picked them up off the sidewalks, out of the gutters, and on the streets. The police brought them to me from hospitals where their mothers rejected them. I rescued them, watched them grow, and made them study.

I found adoptive families for many of them and now they're doing well. They're scattered around the world in America, India, and Europe, but they always remember me. Their adoptive parents send me photographs. In this way I am able to watch my children grow. One is dressed like a cowboy and playing with a toy gun; another is having fun on a sled in the snow in Switzerland or horseback riding in England. I have a big album of their pictures in Calcutta. When I look at it, I always experience great joy because I feel I loved those children as a true mother, just as Jesus taught me to do.

I was also able to arrange many adoptions in India where there are some unique problems. It is a tradition in India that young married couples support the husband's parents, and the husband's parents are the ones who run the household. When their daughter-in-law fails to give them a grandson, they are upset, especially when they're a wealthy family. "We have land, houses, and jewelry," the parents say to their son, "and you don't have any children to whom we can leave our wealth." They encourage their son to leave his wife and to take another so they can have a grandson.

But I've found young husbands who don't want to leave their wives. They come to me for help and I've saved them in many situations using a little trick. A young husband will tell his parents that his wife is pregnant. Then the couple will go on a long vacation, at the end of which they go directly to the hospital where we find them an abandoned newborn baby. They return home with the child as if it were truly their newborn baby and everyone's happy. The unity of many families has been saved in this way and the children that we gave them have grown, finished their studies, and now have important positions in society.

Nevertheless, I haven't been able to find an adoptive family for all the children. Some stay with me. They are the handicapped, mentally retarded, and least desirable. Nature has been cruel to them. But they are God's children and they need love. They are my favorite children.

Once in India I was called to pick up an eight-month-old baby that was abandoned with his five other brothers. His father left the shack where they were struggling to survive before this baby was born. Then his mother died of starvation. He and his brothers were also dying of starvation. Though tiny, he was already hardened by suffering. In fact, he wasn't able to cry. From his filthy little bed full of lice, he looked at the ceiling without moving. It was only after months of loving care that he regained his voice and began to cry.

A lot of the babies we pick up die after a few days. They die because they are too little. Their mothers give birth prematurely, hoping to get rid of them. Some weigh less than two pounds and don't even know how to suck. We try to save them by feeding them through their noses or by building up their strength intravenously. They desperately fight to survive, but often they aren't able to. Often they are poisoned because their mothers take drugs to get rid of them before they're born and the poison passes from the mother to the child.

Many times hospitals tell us that it's useless to pick up such tiny infants because their condition is hopeless. But we still do it. We want them to feel the warmth of love and close their eyes in the arms of someone who loves them in the few hours they still have to live. Every human being suffers when he's not loved, and a tiny baby understands nonetheless and suffers more than any other creature. To refuse him love is like killing him.

In these past few years a new plague has unleashed itself on mankind: AIDS. Everyone's calling it "the plague of the year 2000." It's worse than leprosy. You can protect yourself from leprosy through normal hygienic precautions; it's difficult to protect yourself from the contagion of AIDS. For this reason it's hard to find people who are willing to care for AIDS patients. These poor people are even being abandoned by their own families. But they, too, are God's children and need love. Out of love for God, we are also dedicating ourselves to them. We've already opened two houses in New York for AIDS patients, and two others are in the works.

The children of AIDS victims constitute a particular problem. These children are born with the disease and are immediately surrounded by suspicion and fear and looked upon with horror and hate. They suffer terribly from a lack of love. We want to help them. Right now I'm here in Italy because of this problem. I'm looking for a suitable place where I can open a home to care for babies who are born with AIDS. So far I haven't found anything, but I'm still looking. I'm certain that sooner or later I'll find a benefactor. God will reward that person. These babies are innocent creatures. Because of their illness, their lives will be a hell. We have to do the impossible by relieving them of their suffering and letting them experience God's love for them. We must let them know that they are the Heavenly Father's beloved children precisely because of all their suffering.

# F I F T E E N

# "MY BROTHERS AND SISTERS, THE LEPERS"

When traveling around the world, Mother Teresa always carries a coarse cotton bag containing everything she might need, which is very little. Even though there is nothing of value in that little bag, Mother Teresa cares for it as if it were a family heirloom or a gift from a dearly beloved friend.

The reason why Mother Teresa is so possessive of that little cotton bag is because it was made by her favorite children, the lepers. The material was first woven with extreme difficulty by the maimed hands of one of the thousands of people who are afflicted with this terrible disease, whom she is helping in her numerous leper colonies. The material was then cut out and sewn by other lepers, who are thankful to Mother Teresa because they have been able to find work that is gratifying and that enables them to make a living with dignity.

For ages, leprosy has been feared as the worst thing that can happen to a person. Unlike a cancerous tumor or AIDS, it does not condemn its victims to premature death, but it does condemn them to a sort of "social death." Whoever contracts leprosy is isolated from society and banished by his own relatives. Long ago, lepers were forced to live far away from population centers and wear bells on their feet so healthy people would know they were approaching and flee in terror. Today the bells have been abolished, but society continues to ostracize these people.

According to estimates, there are four million lepers in the world, three million of whom are living in India. In Calcutta, lepers number more than half a million.

Condemned by a disease that frighteningly and progressively deforms their limbs, they are transformed into monsters that people flee and despise. It is impossible for them to find a job and earn a living. Banished from the company of other human beings and even by their own families, lepers are the poorest among the poorest of the poor. For this reason they are people who truly and concretely "represent" Jesus Christ, according to the marvelous faith of Mother Teresa. Therefore, they are the people she wants to "serve" more than any other.

It is an act of utmost heroism to dedicate oneself to caring for lepers with a radical gospel love that sees these people as beloved brothers and sisters. Even among those who practice asceticism, few are able to make such a choice. St. Francis of Assisi took a definitive turn in his conversion experience by embracing a leper. At the height of his experience of "mahatma," Gandhi said that lepers were "God's beloved children." It was inevitable that Mother Teresa would tackle the enormous problem that lepers pose in India after having chosen her mission of total love for the poor in that country.

Mother Teresa did not attempt to do this work at the beginning of her mission, but later when she already had a certain amount of experience. "In 1957," she told me, "five beggars came knocking at our door. They had belonged to middle-class families and had held important positions at work. But when their disease was discovered, they were thrown out and no one wanted to have anything to do with them. They couldn't even return to their families. They were reduced to begging in order to survive. They asked for help, and we received them in our midst. At that time a doctor was coming to help us, Doctor Senn, who instructed a sister in caring for leprosy. Thus, almost by accident, our work with the lepers began."

By 1957 Mother Teresa had eleven years of experience in her work. Her congregation had already been recognized by the Church and had a rule, a structure, and houses. During the years when she was helping poor people in the slums and dying people on the streets of Calcutta, Mother Teresa had various opportunities from time to time to get to know the lepers. She listened to their stories, learned about the conditions in which they lived, and reflected on their problems. She knew they were her beloved brothers and sisters. But being an extremely practical and down-to-earth woman, she also was aware that she needed to be adequately prepared to really love them and help them. When she felt she had precise knowledge of the problem, she went to see what other religious institutes and social service organizations were doing in this area and briefly took some time to objectively evaluate the efficiency of their work. Then she made her own plans.

Her basic idea flowed from her faith and convictions. For Mother Teresa, the lepers were God's children, like all human beings. Jesus died on the cross for them, too. Because of their immense suffering and horrible living conditions, they were participating more than many other Christians in the mystery of the redemptive passion of Jesus that continues within his Mystical Body. "I know," Mother Teresa has affirmed, "that when I touch the limbs of a leper who is giving off a stench, I'm touching Christ's body just as when I receive his body in the sacrament of the Eucharist." In her spiritual vision of the world, lepers were very precious people. As God's children and as human beings, they had a right to dignity, respect, civilized living conditions, the possibility of working, a family, and social relationships—everything that society denies them by ostracizing them and shutting them up in filthy ghettoes.

Mother Teresa began her actual work among the lepers with a trailblazing effort. Various leper colonies existed in Calcutta and in other cities in India. However, only a small number of the people who suffered from this disease could receive care there. The large majority remained at home trying to hide their disease, thereby becoming dangerous sources for contagion. To effectively combat the disease, she needed to search them out.

Mother Teresa knew that near Madras a Belgian doctor, Dr. Hemeryckx, had perfected a method for treating leprosy on a large scale. Using well-equipped, mobile clinics, he was able to treat lepers in their homes and succeeded in reaching a considerable number of victims in this way. This method was practical and effective. So Mother Teresa enthusiastically decided to use it in Calcutta. She spoke to some government doctors about it and convinced them to work with her and her sisters.

These mobile clinics became a specialty of the Missionaries of Charity. The first ones were blessed by Archbishop Perier of Calcutta, who stirred up interest in Mother Teresa's work through his support. Newspaper articles praised her and her work quickly took off. Using these mobile clinics, Mother Teresa's sisters helped tens of thousands of sick people and were able to restore many of them to health.

However, they did not forget about other ways of helping lepers, such as ministering within the traditional leper colonies where the most serious victims could receive care.

One day Mother Teresa heard that the government authorities had decided to expropriate some land on the outskirts of Calcutta in order to construct a new residential zone. One of her leper colonies was in that area, and the authorities were going to force her to close it and move elsewhere since people would never live next to a leper colony.

Mother Teresa was angry. She thought about her lepers and was worried about what would happen to them. She took advantage of the occasion to begin one of her most powerful battles to help the lepers.

She went to the Ministry of Health to plead their cause. Then, with the help of the newspapers, she launched an information campaign and collection called "Leprosy Collection Day." Her sisters and their friends went around the city with boxes bearing a slogan coined by Mother Teresa: "Touch the Leper with Your Compassion." The people's response was overwhelming. Money came in from everywhere. Afterward the government offered Mother Teresa a large piece of land to provide housing for lepers who had been displaced by the new residential area.

In 1958 Mother Teresa opened a large center for lepers in Titagarh, an industrial complex on the outskirts of Calcutta. For a long time the place had been a refuge for lepers. It was a conglomerate of shacks in a swampy area that was home to a host of diseases and pollution that surpassed anything anyone could imagine. Along with leprosy, there was also misery and crime. No one, not even the police, risked venturing into that area, where violence was the norm and where people often committed the most atrocious crimes.

Learning about the problem, Mother Teresa was anxious to visit that ghetto. She saw the horrendous conditions of the poor people there. Disease was rampant, especially among the newborn. With surprisingly rapid decisiveness, she decided that steps should be taken to improve the area and immediately sought ways to provide help. Because of the extremely unhealthy environment and the deep-rooted crime in the area, she entrusted this mission to the male branch of the Missionaries of Charity, which had been recently founded.

As always, the beginnings were difficult. Recalling the great love that Gandhi had for these unfortunate people, Mother Teresa wanted the center there to be called *Gandhiji Prem Niwas,* which means "Gandhi's Gift of Love." The area was disinfected, new streets, housing, a rehabilitation center and a hospital were constructed, and new businesses were opened.

But the crowning achievement of her work for lepers remains *Shantinagar,* "The Place of Peace," a self-sufficient village where lepers live freely without fear of being expelled by the police and without the humiliation of being ostracized by society.

The village is located thirty kilometers from Calcutta, next to the border with Bihar State. The area was once uninhabitable jungle. In 1961, the Governor of Bengal State, B.C. Roy, an important Indian politician, a militant communist but a great admirer of Mother Teresa, wanted to donate thirty-four acres of that jungle to the diminutive nun and her congregation. Mother Teresa, realizing that the area was rich in water, began to cultivate it. Within a few years she had carved out a corner of paradise.

She dreamed of developing a little town in that place for her lepers, and she marvelously succeeded in doing so. Today the jungle is an oasis of greenery with avenues lined by trees and flower beds. There is also a lake that is brimming with fish that provides protein for the inhabitants. Little by little, various buildings have gone up: a rehabilitation center, a hospital, a home for the aged, schools, and many simple, brick houses that blend in with nature.

The town is directed by one of Mother Teresa's sisters. The lepers live in little houses, each housing a nuclear family. They work in shops and in the fields, and raise pigs and chickens. Only the most seriously ill are sent to the hospital. Children who are born there have the advantage of their home and a school, but they also have regular medical checkups in order to discover and immediately stop any possible contagion.

The town is virtually autonomous. In the fields people raise rice, fruit, and vegetables for food. The lepers have also learned to bake bricks for building their houses. Nothing is wasted and everything is recycled. With particular ingenuity, the chicken droppings are transformed into an odorless and colorless gas that is used in the kitchen for cooking. Besides the lepers, many healthy people also live in the village. For the most part they are volunteers who, by their presence and regular contact with the lepers, help ward off any type of ostracism and give the lepers a certain dignity and rights as human beings.

"Lepers," Mother Teresa always maintained, "might look disfigured, but they are marvelous people capable of giving a lot of love, just like the poor."

One day while making a comparison between the sick in India and those in the rich countries of the West, she told me:

Leprosy is without any doubt a terrible disease to have, but not as terrible as feeling unloved, unwanted, or abandoned. Extreme loneliness, which is found among certain people in rich countries, is worse than leprosy. A while ago in New York, a very rich man came to our house. He told me: "Please come and visit me. I'm half blind, my wife is going crazy, our children are traveling around the world and they never think about us. My wife and I are dying of loneliness. We want more than anything to hear the sound of a human voice in our midst." That man lived in a beautiful home and had lots of money, but he was unhappier than a poor leper in India.

# SIXTEEN

# THE CONVENT IN THE CHICKEN COOP

Mother Teresa's work was growing. The Missionaries of Charity were growing in number and their projects on behalf of the sick and the poor were multiplying. The little nun in a white sari who spent her days in the slums was now well known throughout Calcutta. Now even the political authorities appreciated and encouraged her charitable work.

In the early years of her mission, as we have already learned, Mother Teresa became friends with Dr. B.C. Roy, a famous doctor in India who was becoming an increasingly important political figure. He was one of Mahatma Gandhi's collaborators during his campaign of nonviolence for India's independence. He was also a friend of Premier Jawaharlal Nehru and governed Bengal State as chief minister from 1948–64.

Mother Teresa began visiting him to seek medical advice for a person she was helping who was seriously ill but too poor to pay for a doctor. Later she petitioned him for government funds to help the poor people in the slums. Dr. Roy noticed that Mother Teresa was only interested in others. Contrary to his usual experience up to that point, Mother Teresa sought help only for the impoverished and never for people of importance. For this reason, he became curious and decided to get to know Mother Teresa better.

Doctor Roy was a member of the *Brahmo Samaj,* believed in only one God, and deeply respected Jesus Christ and his teachings. He saw Mother Teresa as an extraordinary person who was living the gospel, and he wanted to use all his authority to support her. He was impressed with the efficiency of her first work, *Shishu Bhavan,* the "Children's Home," and officially requested that she open other homes like it. As a result, the attention of the state's political authorities was focused on the work of this humble nun.

The two often had conflicting ideas and quarreled. Since they were both stubborn, neither gave in easily. But their respect for each other helped them eventually to overcome every obstacle.

On his eightieth birthday, Doctor Roy went to his office as usual. There, journalists were waiting to interview him on that special occasion. He reminisced about his life and his work. To everyone's surprise, he did not talk about Gandhi with whom he had fought some important battles, nor did he mention his friend Nehru. But he did remember Mother Teresa: "This morning while I was going up the stairs to my office, I thought about Mother Teresa, who is devoting her life to the well-being of the poor."

The following day, his comments were printed on the first page of every newspaper in Bengal. They drew the attention and admiration of everyone in India to this Catholic nun. They also provoked interest and surprise in Catholic circles.

Rarely, indeed, had such an important Hindu political figure expressed support in this way for a Catholic nun. Missionaries, parish priests, and bishops from various dioceses in India began asking for news about Mother Teresa and her work. Some wrote to her and asked her to send sisters to their dioceses. Mother Teresa had many vocations. It was an opportunity to let people know about her congregation. But the Archbishop of Calcutta reminded her of the rules: no religious congregation could open new houses outside of the diocese where it originated for a period of ten years.

Mother Teresa was in the prime of life. She felt full of spiritual and physical energy. But she had to obey. "The Lord's work shouldn't be hurried," the archbishop told her.

Mother Teresa had received permission to found her congregation in 1950. For ten years, therefore, she worked within the confines of the Archdiocese of Calcutta. But when those ten years were over, she started traveling around India and opening new houses for her sisters, who were in demand everywhere.

The first houses of the Missionaries of Charity opened in Ranchi, Delhi, Jahnsi, and Bombay. Nehru, who was then prime minster of India, took part in the inauguration of the house in Delhi.

However, Mother Teresa was already famous abroad. Many newspapers had written about her and her work. Various countries were asking her and her sisters for help. In order to establish her congregation in other countries around the world, Mother Teresa needed additional ecclesiastical authorizations. The pope needed to declare that the Missionaries of Charity were a pontifical order, canonically dependent on Church authorities in Rome and therefore authorized to operate throughout the Church. But such approval was rarely granted after such a short time. Mother Teresa had to wait.

She was impatient. Her missionary fervor moved her to act. When she went to America for a conference in 1960, she stopped in Rome on the way back. With the help of

Cardinal Gregory Agagianian, she asked Pope John XXIII to declare the Missionaries of Charity a pontifical institute as soon as possible so it could expand worldwide.

Pope John XXIII was already acquainted with Mother Teresa and had a great deal of respect for her work. He listened to her petition and undoubtedly pressed for approval. A letter that he signed and sent to Mother Teresa on October 9, 1962, confirms his interest: "A message from the Holy Father to Mother Teresa. We invoke divine assistance for your worthy apostolate of charity. Continue the good work with your sisters with the paternal apostolic blessing. Signed: John XXIII."

Nevertheless, he was not the one who gave the Missionaries of Charity the long awaited pontifical approval. His successor, Pope Paul VI, did so in 1965. Immediately after receiving this approval, Mother Teresa's sisters began to spread out around the world.

The first house outside of India opened in Cocorote, Venezuela, on July 26, 1965. Immediately afterward another house was opened in Caracas, Venezuela. Other houses followed in Peru, Colombia, Brazil, Bolivia, and Italy, in various countries in Europe, then in Australia, the Middle East, Africa, and some Eastern European countries still under communist rule.

Mother Teresa's work was rapidly expanding. Though appreciated, it encountered difficulties, obstacles, and disappointments. Like every successful work, it provoked envy, jealousy, and rivalry even in Church circles. Some congregations did not look favorably on the growth of the Missionaries of Charity and tried to set up obstacles.

This happened even in Rome. Pope Paul VI himself wanted Mother Teresa's sisters to open a house in the Eternal City. The pope extended his invitation to Mother Teresa when he met her in Bombay in December, 1964, at the 38th International Eucharistic Congress. He immediately sent her a round-trip airline ticket to Rome and $10,000. She went to Italy in 1967. The pope welcomed her with open arms, but some prelates in the Roman Curia remained indifferent. At that time Bishop Paul Hnilica was a great help to her. In August of 1969 she was able to open her first house in Rome. She chose the poorest part of the city, on Via Tor Fiscale near the Appia Nuova, where many people lived in utter misery in shacks and hovels that were falling down. The first house that the Missionaries of Charity opened in Rome was a shack with a metal roof.

From that moment on, street people, abandoned children, and old people who were lonely and tired began to experience the friendship of these extraordinary nuns who, with immense love, showed interest in them and their problems.

Mother Teresa's sisters became popular in Rome. Through their love, sacrificial spirit, and humility, they conquered everyone's heart. Little by little even those in the Roman Curia who were suspicious began to change their minds. The Missionaries of Charity opened another house in San Gregorio al Celio, next to the Colosseum. It was their largest, most beautiful house. For these reasons, perhaps, it annoyed the political forces in Rome, who did not look favorably on the charitable activities of the Church at that time. Toward the end of 1976, when the house was flourishing, Rome's city administration decided to shut it down.

The complex of San Gregorio Magno originated in the seventh century A.D. It is located on the hill of Celio, halfway between the Colosseum and the Circo Massimo. In 1573 it became the property of the Camaldolese monks who used it to house the poor. After Italy was united, the complex was divided in two parts: one, which included the church, some apartments, and other rooms, was reserved for use by the Church; the other was given to the city to be used for social services. At first it housed a children's institute and later, under fascist rule, it became a school for social workers. In 1946 the city gave it back to the Camaldolese monks for use once again in helping the poor.

In 1974 the monks decided to put the complex at Mother Teresa's disposal so that she might transform it as part of her charitable work into a genuine shelter for the poor and abandoned. They advised the city administration about their plans and were authorized to proceed.

Mother Teresa organized an extraordinarily efficient shelter for the homeless in what was an ancient stable. She set up about eighty beds in twenty rooms. Every night the sisters went around the city looking for people desperately in need. Braving wickedness and misunderstanding, they roamed the underground corridors of the main train station, the porticos of the Piazza Esedra, and the ruins of the Colosseum—areas where victims of loneliness and misery generally took refuge. They accompanied the neediest cases to their shelter and helped them with immense love.

In a short period of time, Mother Teresa's work at San Gregorio al Celio became a shining example of Christian love. Even agnostics and atheists were deeply moved when they heard about the marvelous accomplishments of Mother Teresa's sisters. When Augusto Guerriero, a famous Italian columnist, heard about the work in Rome, he wanted to meet Mother Teresa. When he did, he experienced such deep emotions that he started to weep.

Nevertheless, the sisters' loving and unlimited dedication to the poor annoyed some people. When Rome's city administration passed into the hands of the communists, something unexpected happened. On the morning of December 31, 1976, the superior of the Camaldolese Fathers, who had given San Gregorio al Celio to the Missionaries of Charity, received a registered letter from the city council informing him that the sisters' home and their shelter for the homeless would be closed down.

The letter read: "We wish to inform you that this administration absolutely needs to avail itself without any delay of the property that is presently occupied by the order. We request that the said property be free of all persons and things within thirty days of receiving this document, and warn that if these conditions are not fulfilled, action will be taken to protect the rights and interest of the city administration."

It was a genuine eviction notice. It failed to acknowledge everything that Mother Teresa and her sisters had accomplished in two years of intense labor. They showed no consideration for the sisters' heroic sacrifices or for the happiness that they had shared with so many neglected people. "Jesus never abandoned us and won't abandon us now," Mother Teresa's sisters commented peacefully and imperturbably. "He'll show us what to do and will find us another roof under which we can house so many suffering people."

But even if the sisters were resigned to their fate, the people of Rome were not. They gathered in force to support Mother Teresa. Political and religious authorities intervened and the city council was forced to withdraw its eviction notice. The sisters remained at San Gregorio al Celio, where they still carry on their charitable work with the same love and spirit of self-denial.

I met Mother Teresa several times at San Gregorio al Celio. When she was still feeling well, she would regularly come to the Italian capital and almost always stayed at San Gregorio al Celio, the motherhouse for the Missionaries of Charity in Italy.

The first time I entered the building, I was amazed. In that beautiful building dating from Italy's golden age and the former headquarters of the Camaldolese monks, Mother Teresa's sisters had set up a shelter for the homeless. The poor and the abandoned that were picked up at night on the streets of Rome were housed like princes and princesses in a genuine villa.

On the other hand, these religious sisters, these brides of Christ, lived in a chicken coop. It was just that. They transformed an old chicken coop behind the villa into their little convent. It was Mother Teresa who decided to establish the motherhouse of the Missionaries of Charity in Rome in this way.

There they lived in extreme simplicity. There they received their visitors, whether they be famous and powerful figures (such as bishops, cardinals, industrialists, and politicians) or just ordinary people. They offered everyone who came a touching example of absolute poverty.

The convent is clean and pleasant, but it still has the basic elements of a chicken coop. The rooms are small and the walls are plain. There is no insulation in the ceiling, so the rooms are stifling in summer and freezing in winter. There is no heating, even though Rome's cold weather is often overwhelming. A spirit of poverty truly reigns: It is so real and concrete that you have the feeling that you can touch it with your hand. Walking through the corridor that divides the place in two, and realizing that young sisters live in that shacklike structure, you experience a sense of oppression and bewilderment that even the tender but confident smiles on the faces of the nuns cannot dispel.

"We Missionaries of Charity must suffer with Christ,"

Mother Teresa said more than once with complete assurance. "This is the only way we will be in a position to share the sufferings of the poor. Our congregation would die out if our sisters did not walk with Christ in his suffering and if our sisters did not live in poverty. Strict poverty is our safeguard. We do not want to happen to us what happened to other religious orders in the course of history that started out serving the poor and unwittingly ended up serving the rich. To be able to understand and help those who have nothing, we have to live like them. A radical difference lies in the fact that the people we help are poor against their will while we are poor by free choice."

# S E V E N T E E N

# "OUR WEALTH IS POVERTY"

When Mother Teresa traveled, she never carried books, agendas, and briefcases with her. She always traveled the world in complete poverty and evangelical simplicity. Yet she always knew what was going on with her sisters and in her congregation. If someone asked her a question about her large family, she did not need to consult any notes to respond. Everything was clearly written in her mind.

"How many sisters do you have now?" I would ask her at every meeting. She always gave me precise figures that would increase every time.

"Other religious congregations are complaining about a decline in vocations," I observed. "You, on the other hand, don't show any sign of such a crisis."

"The Lord is good to us," she answered. "He is sending us so many vocations, but woe to us if we do not return his good favor with lots of love."

As we have seen, Mother Teresa obtained the Vatican's permission to found the Congregation of the Missionaries of Charity in October, 1950. At that time about ten sisters had joined her. When speaking with me in Rome in 1987, she informed me, "At the present time there are three thousand Missionaries of Charity who live in three hundred fifty houses scattered across eighty nations."

The little seed of her congregation had become a mighty oak. Upon returning from her second heart operation in America in January of 1992, Mother Teresa updated her figures: her sisters now numbered 3,500 in 445 houses across ninety-five nations. During her recovery, she spoke with enthusiasm about China. She had been invited to that country. "As soon as I am able to move about, I have to go to Beijing to open a house there too," she noted. At the time of her death, her sisters numbered 4,500.

Today, Mother Teresa's sisters represent an incredible spiritual movement. While many women's religious institutes have been forced to close various houses because of a lack of vocations, the Missionaries of Charity continue to open houses at a surprising pace.

Every new house means expenses, funds, and investments. The Missionaries of Charity are not a business. They do not open houses to make money. Their work is essentially a service, set up to help the poorest of the poor. Therefore, their work requires money to distribute to those who have nothing. They spend money but do not bring in money. In short, their houses are all losing operations.

Mother Teresa oversaw an enormous army. The 4,500 sisters are responsible for hundreds of thousands of people: poor people, abandoned children, the dying, street people, the handicapped, young unwed mothers, AIDS victims, and lepers. In India alone Mother Teresa's sisters care for 150,000 lepers. They take care of an army of needy people who need housing, food, clothing, and medical care, including costly surgery and medicines that are hard to find.

The overall cost of the operations of the Missionaries of Charity, therefore, involves figures that make most people dizzy and an administrative structure that would give most people a heart attack. Only an extremely wealthy person with an enormous amount of interest income from various bank accounts could calmly face such an enterprise. But Mother Teresa had nothing. Her congregation was founded on poverty—absolute poverty. However, in spite of having nothing, she established a marvelous organization that works perfectly to distribute happiness and hope to thousands and thousands of desperate people. It was an amazing miracle of love for God and faith in God.

It is worth noting that the vow of poverty that the Missionaries of Charity profess is a vow of total poverty, a poverty that seems unthinkable in our times.

The sisters do not possess anything. They live like the people they serve, the poorest of the poor. The rule they scrupulously observe is very strict on this point. The sisters must be poor as individuals and as a community.

Their rule allows a personal wardrobe that is reduced to the essential for each individual sister: a white undergarment that covers her from her neck to her ankles and wrists, with a white sari on top. She wears rough sandals on her feet. Each sister has three undergarments and two saris. When she needs to move, she is ready in ten minutes: everything she possesses fits into a small bag.

The rule also requires that the houses where the sisters reside must be simple and modest and, insofar as possible, resemble those of the poor. In third world countries, the sisters often live in shacks and huts. Out of a spirit of poverty, they also renounce all privacy. They sleep in dormitories without having even a corner for themselves.

"The essential reason for this poverty," Mother Teresa explained, "is out of love. The people we are helping are poor against their will, but our poverty is the fruit of a free choice. We want to be poor like Jesus, who, though rich, chose to be born, live, and work among the poor."

Mother Teresa wanted the vow of poverty to be observed not only by each individual sister but by the congregation itself as a distinct entity. While other religious institutes have a vow of poverty, it concerns only each individual religious. The institute itself may have possessions and income. But this is not the case with the Missionaries of Charity. Even as an entity, they do not possess anything, have any revenue or fixed income, or receive any stipends for the work they do. They live off of charity. Mother Teresa always responded the same way when I asked her about this:

> My work is administered by Divine Providence. It is written in our constitution: "We and our poor will rely completely on Divine Providence. As members of the Body of Christ who lived off of charity during his public life and who served the sick and the poor, we will not be ashamed of begging from door to door."
>
> We possess nothing. Besides the vows of poverty, chastity, and obedience that all men and women religious have in common, we make a special vow to freely serve the poorest of the poor. This vow prohibits us from earning anything from our work. To keep our work afloat, much money is needed. Providence thinks about us by sending it through generous people who wish to work with us. Therefore, we live off of charity, offerings, and alms, little gestures of love on the part of thousands of people.
>
> To show our faith in Providence, we do not accept "fixed" help of any kind, whether it be loans, stipends, or subsidies. I don't even want people to make a commitment to give us a fixed amount of money every week or every month. A fixed income would allow us

to formulate programs, projects, and action plans, but we would no longer be daughters of Providence if we made such concessions.

To have faith in this incredible ideal of evangelical life, Mother Teresa accustomed her sisters to never thinking about tomorrow. As she wrote in the constitution of the congregation: "We must leave every project for the future in the hands of an Omnipotent God because yesterday has gone by, tomorrow is not yet here, and today we only have to know, love, and serve Jesus."

# E I G H T E E N

# "PROVIDENCE WILL NOT FORSAKE US"

As we have seen, Mother Teresa trusted in divine providence alone to run her complex organization.

To most people, the expression "to trust in providence" has become just another expression that has no precise meaning. Indeed, none of us would think of embarking on some huge, costly venture "trusting only in providence" and without having considerable reserves in the bank. We cannot even conceive of people who get involved in such huge ventures without considering the economic risk.

Nevertheless, such people have always existed. They are the saints, whose faith in God is unshakable. "If you have faith, you can move mountains," Jesus tells us in the gospel (see Matthew 17:20). Saints believe this. It seems almost as if they alone have the joy and good fortune of knowing that providence does exist and that God's love for his children is not an abstract expression. As a result, they are the fortunate and grateful witnesses of spectacular miracles.

One day after Mother Teresa had spoken to me about the absolute poverty she wanted her congregation to observe, I said to her: "So then, miracles keep afloat all the work that your sisters are doing throughout the world."

"Precisely," she replied, smiling at the amazed expression on my face. "Every day God works real miracles for us. We see it concretely. If he didn't do wonders for us every day, we couldn't move ahead and we wouldn't be able to do anything."

She looked at me. My amazement was growing. "Are you talking about genuine miracles?" I asked.

"Yes, real miracles," she answered.

Mother Teresa never liked talking, whether in public or in private. In all my meetings with her, I noticed that conversation was always difficult. Being gentle, sweet, and approachable, she was always ready to answer any question, but with short, incisive, and composed sentences. However, whenever the conversation turned to God's goodness, Jesus' love for his children, or the wonders of divine providence, she was very talkative. At those times she would joyfully speak at length.

Providence provides generously for me, my sisters, and the people we're helping. He's done so through industrialists, corporations, businesses, petroleum companies, and governments. But he's especially done so through the small offerings of people of modest financial means. Their offerings have greater value because these people have to sacrifice more to make them and in this way their act is a true act of love.

Providence will never forsake us. My work is what Jesus wanted, and he has to think about keeping it going. Providence continually enables us to experience the love with which Jesus watches over us and helps us.

We always have a state of emergency in our houses on account of everything that is used to support those in need. The sisters who are in charge of running our houses wouldn't be able to sleep peacefully at night if they didn't have immense faith in God. We hardly have what is needed to live for a week and, at times, even what is needed to make it through the evening. But the solution always comes, even if it's at the last moment. The Lord inspires many different people to bring essential aid in different ways and for different reasons. If this help didn't come, we'd be in trouble.

In Calcutta, we cook for nine thousand people every day. One morning a sister came to tell me that we didn't have any more food in the pantry. It was Thursday. The weekend looked bleak. It was the first time that I had to face such a challenge. "We have to warn the people who need help," she said. "No, let's wait," I answered. "Go to the church right away and present this matter to Jesus."

Even I prayed and anxiously waited to see what would happen. At nine o'clock on Friday morning a truck arrived loaded with bread, jam, and milk. It was the supply of food that was intended to be used in the city's school cafeterias. But that morning the government decided to close the schools and God's bounty was no longer needed there. I tried to find out why they closed the schools that morning without any warning, but I could never find out the reason. I believe God intervened to help us. In fact, for two days the people who needed our help were able to eat their fill.

One day a man came to see me. He was crying because his only son was dying. He had taken him to a specialist, who told him that he would be able to save the boy with a special medicine that was very expensive and practically impossible to find in India. Nonetheless, he had written a prescription for his son and the man was asking for my help.

I tried to alleviate his sorrow and told him to remain calm. "We'll bring the medicine from England," I promised. He had hardly left when I realized that I was in a fix. It wasn't easy to get medicine from England, and even if I was able to do so, time was needed and the boy was dying.

While I was thinking about this, one of our helpers arrived as usual with a bag of medicine that he had collected at the homes of the wealthy. We regularly collect medicine that is still good because it is valuable to our poor people who can't buy them. While I was going through the bag, I immediately caught sight of a bottle. It was the medicine that the dying boy needed and it was the exact dose that the specialist had prescribed.

Once, with some other sisters, I was looking for a place where we could open a new house in London. A woman owned a place that corresponded perfectly to our needs. We went to see the owner and, after visiting the house, expressed our desire to rent it. "It will cost £6,500, to be paid immediately," the woman said abruptly. "I don't believe in anything and I don't give charity to anybody." The situation didn't look very promising. We didn't have any funds, but at the same time we needed the house. We decided to go around the city visiting friends and supporters and asking them for their help in an effort to scrape together a good part of the money that was needed. When we met together in the evening, we counted it. We had collected exactly £6,500.

One day a sister called me from Agra, India, asking for fifty thousand rupees to set up a house for abandoned children. "That's impossible," I replied. "Where do you want me to find such a sum of money?" A few minutes later the telephone rang again. It was a newspaper editor. "The Filipino government has presented you with the Magsaysay Award and some money," he announced. "How much?" I asked. "Fifty thousand rupees," he replied. "In that case," I said, "I suppose God wants a children's home to be set up in Agra."

One afternoon, the novice who was in charge of cooking told me that there wasn't any more rice in the pantry. We didn't even have a rupee in the house to buy some. At 4:30 a strange woman came to the door with a bag. "I felt led to bring this to you," she said. The rice that was needed for dinner that evening was in the bag.

On another occasion one of our sisters didn't have any firewood to cook with. There was a big kettle of curry on the stove, waiting to be cooked. As usual, I sent some sisters to pray. After a while the doorbell rang and a benefactor brought us a load of firewood.

During the rainy season, a heavy rain suddenly began to fall in Calcutta. I was worried. I had arranged ninety-five boxes of powdered milk in the courtyard and I knew it would be ruined by the rain. "What should I do, Lord?" I prayed. "The milk is outside." I felt like Jesus wasn't listening because the rain continued to fall steadily and heavily. Then I took a crucifix and carried it in the middle of the boxes of milk, but even this didn't help the rain to stop. After five days, the sky finally cleared up. The boxes were floating in water. We opened them to see if it would be possible to salvage something, and we were greatly amazed to see that the powdered milk was perfectly dry. Some of the wrappers on the boxes were damaged, but not even a drop of water had penetrated the cracks in the wood.

A lot of people are amazed to hear such stories. But there isn't anything extraordinary about them. It's all simple and logical. If I see someone who is poor, I feel a strong desire to help that person. But I'm only a woman. How much stronger is Jesus' desire to help someone in trouble? Blindly believing in his love is sufficient to witness his miracles every day.

Often the Lord helps us in more subtle ways. He inspires people to love us, be nice to us, and help us. But he is the one who is acting on our behalf.

One day two young Hindus visited me and gave me an offering for the poor. Since it was a large sum of money, I asked them where they had obtained it. "We were married a couple of days ago," they answered. "We had set aside a good sum of money for our wedding reception and our parents and our friends gave us more. At the last minute, however, we decided to buy only what was really needed and give you the rest. We love you very much and we thought it would be wonderful to share our love with the poor people you're serving."

Long ago in Calcutta there was a time when sugar was scarce. Word went out around the city that Mother Teresa didn't have any more sugar for her orphans and many people came to our aid. One evening a couple arrived with their six-year-old son. He had a tin can in his hand. For a week the child had refused to eat sugar so he could donate it to those who were less fortunate.

We have coworkers around the world who have formed groups that help us greatly by collecting clothing, bandages, medicine, and all the other things we use in our clinics. The generosity and sacrifices of thousands of people who are unknown to us allow us to help so many people. However, I trust only in prayer. I never think about money. We want to do the Lord's work and he's the one who has to think about how to do it. If he doesn't send what is needed, it means he doesn't want us to do that work.

Those whom I consider my greatest coworkers and my sisters' greatest coworkers are those sick people who are offering their pain to God for us, as well as the contemplative monks and nuns who are praying for my work.

Many sick and handicapped people who can't be involved in any kind of activity are united to us in a true pact of collaboration. They have adopted a sister and are offering their sufferings and their prayers for her. A very deep bond develops between them and they become like one person.

Even I have my "secret collaborator." It is a Belgian woman whom I have known for more than thirty years. Her name is Jacqueline de Decker, and she is very ill. She has had seventeen operations and is offering all her suffering to help me carry out my mission successfully. Every time I have something special to do, she is the one who gives me the strength and courage that I need. In fact, her suffering increases at those times. Sometimes she writes me: "I'm sure that at this time you have a lot to do, a lot of ground to cover, a lot of work, and a lot to say. I know this from the pain that I'm experiencing in my back and from the other sufferings that have become particularly intense."

Jacqueline has never been mistaken. The mysterious bond between our souls enables us to feel what the other is feeling. My bedridden friend is the one who is doing the most difficult part of my work for me.

# NINETEEN

# Holding Mary's Hand

In the numerous books that have been published about her, little is said about Mother Teresa's devotion to the Blessed Virgin. They say that Mother Teresa prayed to Mary, that she never failed to pray the rosary, and that she recommended to her sisters that they have complete faith in the Virgin Mary. But they never describe her devotion in detail. It is almost as though Marian devotion was not a specific characteristic of her spirituality and her work. In my opinion, this is an important, historical oversight. As a result, it obscures a certain aspect of Mother Teresa's spiritual life.

Mother Teresa's devotion to Mary was, in fact, not only intense, strong, loving, and constantly present in her prayers and meditations, but it also constituted one of the fundamental points of her ascetic and mystic ideology, an unwavering ideology that she lived concretely and intensely throughout her life and that she left as an inheritance to her sisters.

Mother Teresa, and her work on behalf of the poorest of the poor, on behalf of those whose lives counted for nothing in the world's eyes because they seemed too insignificant, could be defined as the "pro-life saint."

As she faced every human being, she recalled those supreme truths that guided her. It did not matter to her that the person was a saint or a criminal, an athlete or a leper, a person in power or a person in despair. To her, that person was a child of God for whose eternal salvation Jesus died on the cross. Therefore, that person was to be loved with the same intensity with which God loves them.

These are powerful and disturbing truths that every Christian knows in theory, but which Mother Teresa had rediscovered and revived and applied to her own daily life. This was precisely the secret of her total devotion to the less fortunate people who surrounded her and who were neglected by the world's organizations. Mother Teresa was not concerned solely for the souls of these people who were her brothers and sisters, but also for their bodies. God is Father not only of the soul, but of the whole person: body and soul. Jesus redeems the whole person, and not only the soul. At the end of time, it will be the whole person, body and soul, that will enter into the kingdom of heaven for eternity.

Mother Teresa's "revolution" was to draw attention to the reality of man, to the sacredness of the body of the baptized person, who, as the Church has always taught, is a "temple of the Holy Spirit."

She never forgot that life comes from God and is an expression of God's love. She embodied the passage from the Gospel of St. Matthew in which Jesus summarized what the Christian should do to have eternal life. St. Matthew recalled Jesus' words: "When the Son of Man comes in his glory, and all the angels with him, he will sit upon his glorious throne, and all the nations will be assembled before him,.... Then the king will say to those on his right, 'Come, you who are blessed by my Father. Inherit the kingdom prepared for you, from the foundation of the world. For I was hungry and you gave me food, I was thirsty and you gave me drink, a stranger and you welcomed me, naked and you clothed me, ill and you cared for me, in prison and you visited me.' Then the righteous will answer him and say, 'Lord, when did we see you hungry and feed you, or thirsty and give you drink? When did we see you a stranger and welcome you, or naked and clothe you? When did we see you ill or in prison, and visit you?' And the king will say to them in reply, 'Amen I say to you, whatever you did for one of the least of these brothers of mine, you did for me'" (Matthew 25: 31, 32, 34-40).

Jesus, God incarnate, was the moving force behind Mother Teresa's entire spirituality and ideology, and was the force that inspired all her activity. But Jesus, in his human nature, came to us through Mary, the true Mother of God.

Jesus and his mother, Mary, cannot be separated. Mary is the woman who gave life to Jesus and who made God's incarnation in this world possible. Mary was a true mother to Jesus: she raised him, she educated him, and she guided him in his human life. At the end of her life, specifically through the intervention of her Son who had already risen from the dead, she bodily entered the kingdom of heaven, a sign of the marvelous destiny that awaits every person who lives and dies in Christ.

Mother Teresa was a very concrete and practical woman. She was always aware of God and sought his guidance. Her devotion to and her "agreement" with Mary, the mother of Jesus and the woman who "was assumed into heaven body and soul," were directly proportionate to her faith in and her love for Jesus: extremely strong.

Bishop Paul Hnilica, the Slovak bishop who was Mother Teresa's friend and who knew her very well, told me that her devotion to Mary had origins far back in her life. This devotion was already well developed by the end of her childhood, thanks to her mother. "One time,"

Bishop Hnilica told me, "Mother Teresa confided this to me: 'I always thank my earthly mother and then my true mother, the Blessed Virgin. When I was a little girl in Albania, I would go out walking with my mother and she would tell me, "My child, always let Mary, who is your true mother, guide you. Always try to let her hold your hand, like I'm doing with you right now." Since then I've learned that my true mother is Mary. I've never forgotten this truth in the course of my life, and I've acted accordingly. I've always let myself be guided by my heavenly mother. Before making any decision, I always turn to her, and she has guided me.'"

On another occasion Bishop Hnilica told me: "I've accompanied Mother Teresa on many trips by train, by plane, and by car. We've spent hours and hours together traveling. Mother and her sisters always prayed the rosary during those trips, almost nonstop, in order to be 'in contact' with Mary. When there was an urgent problem that needed to be resolved, all the sisters made a novena to Mary. When Mother Teresa was traveling around the world, her sisters in Calcutta always would make a novena for her. They were powerful and insistent novenas. Her sisters prayed continually—even while driving in the car. The Blessed Virgin, who herself is a mother, couldn't resist their insistent prayers.

"Mother Teresa was convinced that Russia was a missionary territory chosen by Mary. For this reason she wanted to open as many as fifteen of her houses in that country: fifteen like the mysteries of the rosary. When I saw her for the last time before she died, she told me: 'The sisters who are most satisfied with their work are those who work in Russia, under the missionary guidance of the Blessed Virgin.'

"Pope John Paul II blessed a statue of the Virgin of

Fatima back in 1984, and then gave it to Mother Teresa as a gift. She was thrilled and carried that statue back to the motherhouse in Calcutta, where it still can be found."

As these incidents illustrate, Mother Teresa had a deep devotion to the Blessed Virgin.

We have witnessed this devotion elsewhere in this book. When she began her work and successfully opened her first convent, consisting of two rooms in the home of Michael Gomes, her first benefactor, she wanted one of those two rooms, the larger one, to be a little chapel. She placed a little altar against a wall and hung a picture of the Immaculate Heart of Mary above it that she had received as a gift from the Belgian Jesuit, Fr. Van Exen, who was her spiritual director. Mother Teresa had prayed and wept many times in front of that picture during the preceding crucial months. She had "perceived" Mary's help and love while praying in front of that picture. She used to hold that picture with the same love that a person holds their mother's picture. Whenever she moved, she carried it with her, and it is now in the chapel of the motherhouse of the Missionaries of Charity in Calcutta.

Whenever she told the story of her congregation, she always made it a point to say that the document from the Holy See that officially recognized her congregation arrived in Calcutta on October 7, the Feast of Our Lady of the Rosary. She believed that the coincidence was a sure sign of Mary's benevolence.

The letters that Mother Teresa sent to her friends during that time in her life abound with references to the Blessed Virgin: "Pray to our Lady for me; ask Mary to send us sisters. Don't forget to put in a good word for me to Mary."

Mother Teresa's writings contain endless references to the Blessed Virgin, and to the importance of living unceasingly in communion with the Mother of Jesus:

"I believe that if Jesus was able to listen to Mary, then we, too, should be able to listen to her. She was there, under the cross, sharing in Jesus' passion. She continually enters into our life and the life of the world to bring joy and peace and to turn us to God.

"I am only a small instrument in God's hands. Our Lord and our Blessed Lady gave all glory to God the Father. Following their example, I, too, in a very, very little way, am trying to give all glory to God the Father.

"We ask the Virgin Mary to make our heart like the heart of her Son. How much we can learn from Mary! She was humble because she gave herself entirely to God.

"We ask the Blessed Virgin to give us her heart—so pure, so beautiful, so spotless, so full of love and humility—in order to receive Jesus and love him in the suffering disguise of the poorest of the poor.

"The Virgin Mary will teach us humility. Though full of grace, she declared herself a servant of the Lord. Like her, let us not be ashamed and let us not hesitate to do the most lowly jobs. Like her, let us always accept the cross in whatever form it presents itself.

"Even the Virgin Mary showed complete faith in God, willing to be used as an instrument, an object, for his plan of salvation.

"It is difficult for us to understand Jesus because he is God. Mary, on the other hand, is definitely one of us.

"Love Mary unconditionally and trust her completely.

"Do you know why we ought to love Mary so much? Because she was the spotless image of God's love.

"We learn from Mary, who was Jesus' teacher when he was a child. Like her, let us be attentive to everyone's needs: material and spiritual.

"Let us ask Mary to come into our lives and to make

the "electrical current," that is, Jesus, run through us and enter the world, joining together the hearts of all men and women.

"If Mary and Joseph were looking today for a place to shelter Jesus, would they choose our homes with all their clutter? Do our homes and do our lives reflect the simplicity of Bethlehem?

"You and I were created for the same purpose, to love and to impart that love everywhere and at all times, just like Mary. Like Mary, we, too, ought to search for our children, just like she did when Jesus was lost."

It is almost possible to say that all of Mother Teresa's writings and all of her speeches contained some reference to Mary, whether it be to pray to her, to imitate her, to love her, or to invoke her counsel and help.

As I have already pointed out, Mother Teresa was a very practical woman. For this reason, she was always looking for concrete results in her spiritual life, in her relationship with God. Her faith was never truncated from the realities of life. If she had any material needs or problems, she prayed intensely so that God would help her in some precise way. Her faith in the fatherhood of God was elementary: "God is my Father, therefore he wishes the best for me and helps me." Likewise was her faith in Mary: "Mary is a mother, therefore she understands me, knows my problems, and knows how wonderful it is to receive help. I pray to her because I'm sure she will help me."

Her prayers were dictated by this practical spirit in which the certainty of being heard was an expression of total love.

Mother Teresa, being the practical person she was, also cultivated those concrete symbols and signs that help us to be in contact with the people we love. She kept pictures of the children she had saved and put up for adoption. She was deeply attached to her rosary, which she held in her hands during long "conversations" with the Blessed Virgin every day and at several times during the day. And she had an enormous devotion to the "Miraculous Medal." This is a very special medal whose origins date back to 1832. It is a medal that Saint Catherine Laboure had made at the explicit request of the mother of God.

Catherine Laboure, a French woman born in 1806, entered the Congregation of the Sisters of Charity at the age of 24, an order of nuns founded by St. Vincent de Paul. While she was a novice in Paris, she had three visions of the Blessed Virgin. The first one occurred on the night of July 19, 1830. As she herself described it, she was awakened by her guardian angel who told her to go to the church in the convent where Mary was waiting for her. She went there and saw a majestic woman, seated on a chair next to the altar.

The second apparition took place on November 27 of the same year. The Virgin Mary, who always appeared to Catherine in the convent's church, was standing, clothed in a white silk dress, a white veil, and a silverish blue cape. Her feet rested on a partially illuminated globe and were crushing a green serpent with yellow spots. Her arms were extended and her hands gave off rays of light. The Blessed Virgin entrusted Catherine with the task of making a medal of this apparition and promoting it.

The young novice told her confessor about these two visions, but he did not believe her. A few weeks later, Mary appeared to Catherine for a third time, and scolded her because she had not yet had the medal made. Catherine once again spoke with her confessor, who sent her to the bishop this time, and Mary's desire was fulfilled.

In 1832 people began to distribute the medal. It

quickly acquired the name of "Miraculous Medal" because of the numerous miracles and healings attributed to it. Since then, millions and millions of copies of this medal have been distributed.

Mother Teresa was a big promoter of this medal. She always carried several with her, and distributed them to everyone. She often gave someone she just met a Miraculous Medal as a gift. She would take it in her hands, pray silently, and then offer the small object as a gift.

These were extraordinary gifts. Everyone who met Mother Teresa knew that they had just received a precious gift. Not only had she "personalized" it when she took it between her hands and prayed for the person receiving it, but her gesture was also an act of love that gave birth to some sort of indelible bond. Mother Teresa "bonded" herself to that person in some mysterious way, and considered that person a spiritual son or daughter and a co-worker.

Thousands and thousands of people around the world have received a Miraculous Medal from Mother Teresa's hands. Now that she has died and is in paradise, she certainly is protecting these people. That medal now constitutes a bond between them and Mother Teresa. She gave it as a gift, asking the Virgin Mary to protect that person. Now she will certainly continue to intercede for that person, and her prayer will be even more effective.

The medals that Mother Teresa gave out have an important spiritual value. I, too, have one. One evening Mother Teresa noticed that I was wearing a gold chain around my neck. She took a small medal out of her pocket, held it between her hands, prayed, and then asked me to fasten it to that chain. Since then I have never taken it off. I know that it protects me, that it has helped me a lot, and that it concretely fulfills its role as a "bond" with Mother Teresa, who gave it to me, and with Mary, to whose care Mother Teresa entrusted me.

There is a person in Trieste, Italy, who has received an extraordinary grace through the medal that Mother Teresa gave him as a gift. His name is Remo Gessi and he is a colleague, insofar as he, too, is a journalist.

I met Remo Gessi a few months after Mother Teresa's death. He was at his country home, in the village of Muggia, just two kilometers from Italy's border with Slovenia.

He is an athletic and extremely kind man. While chatting with him, I found out that he belongs to a prominent Italian family. His great-grandfather was Romolo Gessi, a famous explorer. In the nineteenth century Romolo Gessi and his friend and colleague, Gordon Pasica, carried out several historic expeditions in the Sudan. His grandfather, Felice, was also an explorer. Remo Gessi has one son, who is named after his great-great-grandfather and who is an orchestra director. He also has two daughters, Paola and Federica, who have graduated from college and are now married. Before their marriages, they were both well-known television celebrities in Italy.

The reason why I went to see him was to find out the real story behind a healing he had experienced, which took place after meeting Mother Teresa. Specifically, I wanted to know whether he felt like he was one of Mother Teresa's "miracles."

"'Miracle' is a word I don't use," Remo Gessi answered, becoming serious and prudent. "Only the Church can declare a miracle. In general the Church does so only after a long process to verify it. In my case, we'll see what happens in the future. What really happened is this: Mother Teresa changed my physical and spiritual life. If I hadn't met her, I wouldn't be here to tell you about her."

Sitting there in the sun, in the garden of his beautiful house overlooking the enchanting, blue Adriatic Sea, he told me his story:

"When I met Mother Teresa in June of 1988, I was in the midst of a crisis. Because of a tumor, the doctors had given me only a few months to live. My morale was low. But Mother Teresa quickly changed everything.

"The whole episode began in the summer of 1983. I noticed that I had a spot on my right arm, a couple of inches below my shoulder. It didn't look good to me. I went to my doctor in Trieste, who told me it was an age spot. 'It's probably nothing,' he said. Nonetheless, he was careful enough to do some further tests to see if it might be a benign or malignant melanoma.

"I had some lab tests done in Trieste, but the results weren't conclusive. They told me that there was a fifty-fifty chance that it was a malignant melanoma. At that point, I went to the leading Italian specialist in the area, Dr. Natale Cascinelli, at the Tumor Clinic in Milan, who determined that, indeed, it was without any doubt a malignant melanoma. He operated on me December 3, 1983.

"The operation seemed successful, so much so that Dr. Cascinelli didn't give me any further treatment. He told me that we caught it in its earliest stages and that the timeliness of the operation had averted any complications.

"Four years later, however, the disease reappeared. In the intervening time, I hadn't taken any precautions. I continued to go out in my boat, swim, and sunbathe, like I always had. In 1987 I began to feel an itch on my arm and some swelling. I went right away to Milan, and Dr. Cascinelli operated on me again. He told me that I had experienced a relapse and that it had metastasized. I was scared, and the doctor also seemed very concerned. In fact, within three months, I was in trouble again. The cancer appeared in other places, and I was operated on once again. But it was in vain. The cancer spread to my neck, back, chest, and abdomen. I underwent another operation that didn't do anything.

"At that point, Dr. Cascinelli advised me to go to America to see an expert in the field, Dr. Baltch. It was then that I met Mother Teresa.

"Even though I was very sick, I continued to work. I travelled a lot. One day, when I was taking the plane from Ronco dei Legionari to Rome, I met Mother Teresa. She had been in Udine for a conference, and I happened to be seated next to her on her return trip.

"Before the plane took off, people were continually approaching her, greeting her, shaking her hand, and asking her to pray for their sick friends. I couldn't help but overhear, but the thought never occurred to me, not even for a moment, to tell her about my illness.

"When the plane took off, I remained seated next to her and we began to talk in English. We spoke about the conference that she had been at in Udine. However, she read my heart and noticed that I was worried. Looking into my eyes, she asked, 'What's going on?' Then I told her about my problem. She wanted me to tell her the whole train of events. I told her about the disease, the operations, and the trip I was going to make to Houston. She listened attentively. At the end, she told me 'to have faith,' and 'to act,' the usual things that people say in such situations. Then, acting as though she had some unexpected inspiration, she turned to the nun who was sitting next to her and asked her for something. The sister gave her a medal. She put it between her hands, closed her eyes, and silently prayed for almost a minute. Then she gave me the medal and said, 'Put it around your neck and never take it off. Let's expect that our Blessed Lady will perform a miracle for you.'

"She used that very word 'miracle.' While later reflecting on it, it occurred to me that she had perfectly understood the seriousness of my illness. It was a fact that at that point the doctors could do nothing more after three surgeries. My body was full of metastases. They would remove one from one place and another would appear elsewhere. It's strange that she said, 'Let's expect that our Blessed Lady will perform a miracle for you.' Yet it was clear that only a miracle could save me.

"When we arrived in Rome, I said goodbye to Mother Teresa, but I suddenly realized that my contact with her had changed my life. When I returned home, I immediately put the medal that she gave me around my neck. And I did so full of faith, a faith that she had 'transfused' into me. I wasn't the same as before. My wife, Nadilla, also perceived it right away. I wasn't depressed anymore. I found strength to fight again, and at the same time a strange peacefulness. I no longer thought about death. I only had a deep desire to live a good, peaceful life. How long didn't matter anymore.

"I decided to do everything that the doctors had advised me to do, but I did it with complete indifference, as if I were totally healthy. I went to Houston and saw Dr. Baltch, who prescribed a course of treatment. I travelled around the United States for a month with my wife because I wanted to take a vacation with her. When I returned to Italy, I had the treatment that was prescribed, while continuing to live as if I were healthy, without the least bit of worry. The impossible happened. The illness was arrested. The various metastases vanished. The lymph glands in my body had been grossly swollen, but little by little the swelling went down, until they were almost invisible. Every six months, I went to see the doctors for an exam, and they looked at me surprised. Everything had changed. The illness regressed and no longer bothered me.

"Was it Mother Teresa? Was it the treatment that Dr. Baltch prescribed? It's difficult to say. I only know that the treatment didn't do anything for the other people who were with me in Houston. Unfortunately they died within a short time. I, on the other hand, am still alive. Nine years have gone by. I'm so healthy, it's like I never had that disease.

"But looking beyond my physical condition, which is already a matter of great importance, there's my psychological, spiritual, and moral condition. I'm a changed man. I've become a happy person, full of enthusiasm and joy. That's the true and authentic miracle that Mother Teresa did for me.

"I never met Mother Teresa again. But since that meeting long ago, I have never failed to wear the medal she gave me. I don't wear it out of superstition, but as a symbol of her protection, just as people carry around photos of their spouses, children, or parents. I've always felt Mother Teresa's protection through that medal. Last year when I was with some friends near Piacenza, I was bit by a hornet. I had an allergic reaction and went immediately to the emergency room where I went into shock. Before passing out, I kissed the medal that Mother Teresa had given me, and then lapsed into a coma. Later the doctors told me they gave me resuscitation and that they were able to save me only through a miracle. But I'm convinced that, if she hadn't intervened on my behalf, probably even that 'miracle' wouldn't have happened. Mother Teresa is close by me. Now that she's dead, I feel it even more."

Remo Gessi's story is a beautiful and moving story. But there are many others like it. Everyone who has met Mother Teresa has received many blessings from her, whether they be material blessings or spiritual blessings. Her presence alone was an irresistible testimony of the divine reality through which the universe exists. With a few words or a simple gesture, she made us feel Jesus' presence and Mary's presence. "Be everything for Jesus alone, through Mary," she often wrote to those who asked her for her autograph.

# TWENTY

# Her Secret

I have finally come to the end of this little book. I planned on telling the story of Mother Teresa of Calcutta and I believe that task has been fulfilled, even if briefly.

I say "briefly" because my research had to be limited to that which everyone sees and is in the public domain. Mother Teresa was good, kind, and available, but jealous of her private life. She could not hide the facts and dates about her public life and work, but she was very discreet about the rest. However, even this biographical sketch is sufficient to help people understand that this small, amazing nun was one of the great heroes of our time.

From a worldly point of view, she did not accomplish anything sensational. She did not make any scientific discoveries to improve mankind's existence; she did not vanquish the wars that throw the geography of nations into confusion; she did not subjugate or dominate people; she did not build cities, monuments, or cathedrals.

Born in a little city in Kosovo, she was a normal, happy child. When she was eighteen years old, she became a nun so she could be a missionary to India. But her superiors sent her to teach in a girls' high school in India and her life was completely hidden and anonymous until she was thirty-six. Then Mother Teresa felt a call to absolute poverty. She left her religious community and became a beggar among the poorest of the poor in Calcutta, the world capital of misery.

It seemed like an insane, senseless, and utopian choice that would ultimately destroy this poor woman's life. But it was a choice "guided" by a light on high and put into practice with immense love. A miracle occurred in Mother Teresa whereby a divine explosion produced a force that was magnetic and irresistible. In a short period of time, people began to notice that this frail, wrinkly nun from Calcutta was a treasure in today's world and had lighted a fire that was becoming a light in the universe. Over the years Mother Teresa received many awards and was highly acclaimed. Important magazines have dedicated their covers to her as they do to movie stars, royalty, sports champions, and world leaders. She was even honored with the highly prestigious Nobel Peace Prize. International movements grew up around her, made up mostly of young people. Mother Teresa became a symbol, a truly great hero who left her mark on the history of our time, a mark that will become sharper with time.

I want to close this book with a prayer. Mother Teresa was famous for her original, nonconformist prayers full of poetry. She wrote so many that they have been collected and published in various books and highlighted in television documentaries. This prayer, however, was not composed by her. It was written by St. Francis of Assisi at the beginning of the second millennium. Thus it is old, almost eight hundred years old, yet it is still relevant. People like Mother Teresa who have had the mystical experience of an overwhelming encounter with God know it. It is for this reason that she liked this prayer very much. She recited it often and took advantage of every opportunity to share it with others. When asked to speak about herself and her work, Mother Teresa quickly found a way to bring up this prayer by St. Francis, almost as if to indi-

cate that these words written by the saint from Assisi contain the secret philosophy that inspired her every act. Here
is the prayer:

> Lord, make me an instrument of your peace:
> where there is hatred, let me sow love;
> where there is injury, pardon;
> where there is discord, unity;
> where there is doubt, faith;
> where there is error, truth;
> where there is despair, hope;
> where there is darkness, light;
> where there is sadness, joy.
>
> O divine Master, grant that I may seek not so much
> to be consoled as to console,
> to be understood as to understand,
> to be loved as to love.
> For it is in giving that we receive,
> it is in losing ourselves that we find ourselves,
> it is in pardoning that we are pardoned,
> it is in dying that we are born to eternal life.

# BIOGRAPHICAL NOTES ON MOTHER TERESA

1910      August 27: Mother Teresa of Calcutta is born in Skopje, an Albanian city in Kosovo, that will come under Yugoslavian rule a few years later. She is born into a happy and wealthy Catholic family. At baptism, she is given the name of Agnes. Her family calls her "Gonxha," which means "flower bud." Her father, Nicola Bojaxhiu, a wealthy businessman with a degree in pharmacy, and her mother, Drone, a young and beautiful woman, have a daughter, Agatha, who is three years old, and a son, Lazar, who is two years old.

1919      June: Nicola Bojaxhiu dies at the age of forty-six, presumably at the hands of the Yugoslavian police. He was a city councilor who was active in a movement whose aim was to annex Skopje to Albania.

1922      Agnes hears some Jesuit missionaries who are working in India preach in her parish church, and feels the desire for the first time to consecrate her life to God by becoming a missionary. But, as she herself would later admit, she did not want to become a nun, so she let the matter drop.

1928      Agnes is eighteen years old, has finished school, and is thinking about her future. Reading letters from Jesuit missionaries in India, she again feels an inner voice inviting her to become a missionary to India. This time she seriously considers the matter. Since the only way her dream can come true is by entering a religious order of missionary sisters, she chooses the Congregation of Our Lady of Loreto that has a mission in the Bengal province of India.

     September 25: Agnes leaves her family and travels to Dublin, Ireland, where the motherhouse of the Congregation of the Sisters of Our Lady of Loreto is located.

     December 1: After spending two months at the motherhouse of the Sisters of Loreto, Agnes leaves for India.

1929      February: Arriving in Calcutta, Agnes continues on to Darjeeling, a city on the slopes of the Himalayas where the Sisters of our Lady of Loreto have their novitiate. She officially begins her religious life by wearing the religious habit and taking the name of Sister Teresa, out of devotion to St. Thérèse of the Child Jesus.

1931      January 24: Having finished her two years of novitiate, Sister Teresa makes her preliminary vows. She leaves Darjeeling for her new assignment: the high school that the Sisters of Our Lady of Loreto run in Calcutta, where she studies for her teaching certificate and teaches history and geography.

1934        May 24: She makes her final vows within the congregation and becomes the principal of the Bengali section of her school.

1946        September 10: During a train trip to Darjeeling where she will be making a retreat, she is suddenly struck by the extremely miserable conditions of the poor. She hears a call to leave her congregation and devote herself entirely to serving the poor.

            October: Returning to Calcutta, she confides in her superior about her desire. Her superior considers it absurd. Sister Teresa insists and encounters hostility and suspicion in her congregation. She suffers because of it and falls ill. However Archbishop Ferdinand Perier of Calcutta has a sense that this nun will accomplish a major plan of divine providence and decides to help her.

1948        February 2: Having examined Sister Teresa's new spiritual desire at length, Archbishop Perier writes to Pope Pius XII asking his permission for her to leave the Loreto Sisters and begin a new religious life outside of the convent.

            June 6: Pius XII answers Archbishop Perier's letter and grants Sister Teresa permission to continue to be a sister outside of the convent.

            August 16: Sister Teresa turns in her habit as a Sister of Loreto and leaves the convent.

            September: Sister Teresa goes to the Medical Missionary Sisters' Hospital at Patna, founded by Mother Dengel, and takes a nursing course that will better prepare her to serve the poorest of the poor.

December: Sister Teresa returns to Calcutta and chooses December 25, Christmas Day, as the day when she officially begins her new mission of serving the poorest of the poor.

1949      March 19: On the Feast of St. Joseph, Sister Teresa welcomes her first sister in her new congregation, Shubashini Das. Spiritually, she is now a "mother:" Mother Teresa.

1950      January: Mother Teresa already has ten women working with her. Following Archbishop Perier's suggestion, she writes a rule for the religious order she wants to establish. The archbishop examines the draft she has prepared and then sends it to Rome.

October 7: The Vatican's reply arrives approving Mother Teresa's new congregation of sisters that will be called the "Missionaries of Charity."

1952      Mother Teresa founds her first social work on a large scale, *Nirmal Hriday*, the Home for the Dying.

1954      She opens *Shishu Bhavan*, the Children's Home.

1961      She establishes *Shantinagar*, the Lepers' Village.

1960      October: She leaves India for the first time, going to America to take part in a congress. On her way back, she stops in Rome and goes to the Vatican where, with the help of Cardinal

Gregory Agagianian, she presents Pope John XXIII with a request that the Congregation of the Missionaries of Charity be recognized as a pontifical institute.

1963    September: Mother Teresa's work continues to develop and is admired worldwide. The President of India presents her with the Padmashree Award, and the President of the Philippines grants her the Magsaysay Award.

March 25: The Archbishop of Calcutta approves the male branch of Mother Teresa's work, the "Missionary Brothers of Charity."

1964    December: Pope Paul VI meets with Mother Teresa during his trip to Bombay and expresses his appreciation for her work by donating an expensive automobile that he received as a gift from the faithful in the United States.

1965    February 1: Paul VI grants Mother Teresa's congregation pontifical approval.

July 26: Mother Teresa goes to Venezuela where she founds her congregation's first house outside of India in the city of Cocorote.

1967    December 8: She opens a house in Colombo, Sri Lanka.

1968    August 22: She opens her first center in Rome.

September 8: She opens a center in Tabora, Tanzania.

1969    March 26: Paul VI approves the "Association of Co-Workers of Mother Teresa."

September 13: Mother Teresa opens a center for the Aborigines in Bourke, Australia.

| | |
|---|---|
| 1970 | April 26: She opens a center in Melbourne, Australia |
| | July 16: She opens a house in Amman, Jordan. |
| | December 8: She inaugurates the novitiate for the Missionary of Charity in London. |
| 1971 | January 6: She receives the John XXIII Peace Prize in Rome, which is conferred on her by Pope Paul VI. |
| | September: She receives the Good Samaritan Award in Boston, Massachusetts. |
| | September 16: She receives the John F. Kennedy International Prize in New York. |
| | October: She is given an honorary doctorate in Washington, D.C. |
| | October: She opens a house in Belfast, Northern Ireland, and in the Bronx, New York. |
| 1972 | September 15: The government of India awards her the Pandit Nehru Award for International Understanding. |
| 1973 | April 25: Prince Philip of England confers on her the Templeton Prize for Progress in Religion. |
| | October 20: In Milan, Italy, she takes part in the walk of solidarity and receives the Ambrogino d'Oro Award. |
| 1975 | The United Nations Food and Agricultural Organization awards her the Albert Schweitzer Prize. |
| | December 29: *Time* magazine dedicates its cover to her, with the headline, "Living Saints: Messengers of Love and Peace." |

1976    January 17: The French weekly, *Paris Match,* dedicates its cover to her.

August 6: She addresses the 41st Eucharistic Congress in Philadelphia, Pennsylvania.

1979    March 1: President Pertini of Italy gives her the 1978 Balzan International Prize in Rome.

October 17: She receives the Nobel Peace Prize in Oslo, Norway.

1980    January 25: She receives the highest award of the government of India, called the *Bhjarat Ratna,* or *Jewel of India.*

1981    May: She receives an honorary degree from the School of Medicine of the Catholic University of the Sacred Heart in Rome, Italy.

1983    August: Mother Teresa recuperates in the hospital after receiving a pacemaker.

1988    February: She goes to Moscow and receives permission from the communist authorities to open a house in the Soviet capital.

1990    March: After several heart attacks, she presents her resignation as Superior General of her congregation.

September 8: The general chapter of her congregation unanimously reelects her as Superior and she accepts.

1991    March: She returns to her native land, Albania, where she takes part in the inauguration of the cathedral in Tirana, which was converted into a movie house under the communist regime, and opens three houses for charitable work.

| | |
|---|---|
| 1992 | In Calcutta she meets Diana, Princess of Wales, who is undergoing a critical period in her life. Mother Teresa urges her to devote herself to voluntary service and a friendship begins between the two women. |
| 1993 | She contracts malaria in India. |
| | She is hospitalized at the Birla Heart Research Centre in Calcutta for another serious heart attack and she receives a second pacemaker. |
| 1996 | May 21: Mayor Francesco Rutelli names her an Honorary Citizen of Rome at a ceremony in Rome's Campidoglio. |
| | August 20: She is hospitalized at the Woodlands Hospital in Calcutta for an umpteenth cardiac crisis. Doctors disclose that she has tested positive for malaria, which she contracted in 1993. |
| | November 26: Following another heart attack, she is hospitalized in Calcutta. She says, "Let me die like my poor ones." |
| | November 29: She undergoes a coronary angioplasty in New Delhi. |
| 1997 | March: For the third time she resigns as Superior General of her congregation. Her resignation is accepted and Sister Nirmala Joshi is elected as her successor. |
| | June: Her last meeting with her friend, Princess Diana, in the Bronx in New York. |
| | June 29: Her last meeting with Pope John Paul II in Rome. |

September 1: Back in Calcutta, she receives the tragic news of Princess Diana's death. She professes her profound sadness and her desire to pray for her friend the princess.

September 5: At 9:30 P.M. while she is in her room getting ready for bed at the motherhouse of her congregation, she has a heart attack and dies.

September 6: News of Mother Teresa's death is reported by the mass media around the world. Grief is widespread and deep.

September 7: Pope John Paul II, before reciting the Angelus on television while at his summer residence in Castelgandolfo, commemorates Mother Teresa at length, calling her, among other things, "a dearest sister," and holding her up to believers as "an eloquent example."

September 9: Cardinal Joseph Ratzinger speaks about Mother Teresa during a press conference and says, among other things: "I think in Mother Teresa's case the process of beatification can move ahead very quickly since her life was so resplendent."

September 13: A state funeral, attended by heads of state, rulers, and other famous personalities from many nations, is held for her in Calcutta and is televised around the world. That afternoon she is buried at the motherhouse of her congregation.